My Friendship with
Martin Buber

Judaic Traditions in Literature, Music, and Art
Harold Bloom and Ken Frieden, *Series Editors*

My Friendship with

Martin Buber

Maurice Friedman

Syracuse University Press

Quotations from correspondence between Maurice Friedman and Martin Buber
are reprinted by permission of The Martin Buber Estate.

∞ The paper used in this publication meets the minimum requirements of the American
National Standard for Information Sciences—Permanence of Paper for Printed Library
Materials, ANSI Z39.48-1992.

For a listing of books published and distributed by Syracuse University Press,
visit our website at SyracuseUniversityPress.syr.edu.

ISBN: 978-0-8156-1016-8

Library of Congress Cataloging-in-Publication Data

Friedman, Maurice S.

My friendship with Martin Buber / Maurice Friedman. — First edition

pages cm

Includes bibliographical references and index.

ISBN 978-0-8156-1016-8 (cloth : alk. paper)   1. Buber, Martin, 1878–1965.   I. Title.

B3213.B84F75 2013

296.3092—dc23

[B]   2013008843

Manufactured in the United States of America

To Eugenia

My greatest support and my most meaningful relation during the last five years have been with my wife Eugenia. Although we discovered during our first two years together very serious problems in our personalities that made our relationship difficult and often unhappy, we have succeeded in working most of them out. Despite the great strain in which we have lived during the last two years, we have noticed a marked improvement in our relationship and a growing maturity in our personalities. Eugenia shares with me my feeling for the "I-Thou" relationship, and we help each other grow in awareness of its implications for our lives.

Maurice Friedman to Martin Buber, July 25, 1950

MAURICE FRIEDMAN was professor emeritus of religion, philosophy, and comparative literature at San Diego State University. He almost single-handedly introduced the work of Martin Buber in the United States with his 1955 book *Martin Buber: The Life of Dialogue* and with his translations of Buber's *Eclipse of God, The Knowledge of Man, Hasism and Modern Man, The Origin and Meaning of Hasidism,* and *Meetings.* He is the author of over twenty books, including *Martin Buber's Life and Work* (three vols.); *Encounter On the Narrow Ridge: A Life of Martin Buber; Martin Buber and the Eternal; Touchstones of Reality;* and *Abraham Joshua Heschel: Philosopher of Wonder.*

KENNETH PAUL KRAMER is professor emeritus of comparative religious studies at San José State University, California, where he taught from 1976 to 2001. He holds a BA from Temple University, a BD from Andover Newton Theological School, an STM from Yale Divinity School, and a PhD (1971) in religion and culture from Temple University. He has published *Learning Through Dialogue: The Relevance of Martin Buber's Classroom* (2013); *Martin Buber's Spirituality: Hasidic Wisdom for Everyday Life* (2012); *Redeeming Time: T. S. Eliot's "Four Quartets"* (2007); and *Martin Buber's "I and Thou": Practicing Living Dialogue* (2003). He is also the editor of *Dialogically Speaking: Maurice Friedman's Interdisciplinary Humanism* (2011).

Contents

Foreword

KENNETH P. KRAMER

A person does not spend his entire life polishing a single lens unless doing so quickens his awareness, hones his perspectives, and releases a continuity of significant discoveries. Not shackled by the imperatives of classical pedagogy, Professor Maurice Friedman's intellectual career, which spans sixty years of study, teaching, writing, speaking, traveling, mentoring, and cofounding the Institute for Dialogical Psychotherapy, has engendered grammars of genuine dialogue. With illuminating range, he has applied Martin Buber's philosophy of dialogue to the human sciences, asking not only what we know but also how we come to know. Viewed from the standpoint of a Jewish philosopher writing as a philosophical anthropologist, Friedman's central subject has been the I-Thou relationship, an alternative way of knowing beyond individualism and collectivism. This foundation of Buber's work, according to Friedman's concluding sentence in his introduction to Buber's culminating work, *The Knowledge of Man* (1965), "refers us with a profundity unequaled in our time to [our] still unfathomed relation to being and meaning."[1]

Clearly, as this book shows, Martin Buber was the most deeply intellectual and spiritual presence in Friedman's life. Although Friedman never studied formally with Buber, through Buber Friedman came to a deep concern with Hasidism, biblical

Judaism (the Hebrew Bible), psychotherapy, education, social philosophy and social problems, existentialism, and the life of dialogue—all of which he has expressed in his writing and teaching over the years. What Friedman especially inherited from Buber was a profound caring about the question of how best to respond to each person's unique address with one's wholeness of being. A dialogically interhuman response to the immediate requires deep inner intention, which the Hasidim called *kavana*. Buber's life gave Friedman one such expression of authentic dialogue, which, as Buber wrote, is "a part of our birthright as human beings, for only through it can we attain authentic human existence."[2] For this reason, Friedman wrote in his one-volume biography of Buber, *Encounter on the Narrow Ridge*, "In a time when we are in danger of losing our birthright as human beings, Martin Buber has given us again an image of the human."[3]

Although Friedman did not meet Buber until after six years of immersion in his work, their first face-to-face encounter—on October 31, 1951, at the Hotel Marcy on Ninety-sixth Street in New York City—was both memorable and instructive for Friedman. Buber, who was staying in New York while teaching at the Jewish Theological Seminary, welcomed Friedman by looking deeply into his eyes while taking his hand. Friedman's initial response was to feel how totally "other" Buber seemed. His eyes were of a depth, gentleness, and directness that Friedman had never before encountered. Indeed, in 1961, a year after Friedman had spent four months in Jerusalem with Buber, he asked himself, "What did I experience when I looked into Buber's eyes?" Upon reflection, Friedman realized that when he looked into Buber's eyes, he understood that Buber really included him and, for this very reason, also placed a demand on him to be fully present. This was by no means an easy demand!

In this first encounter Buber told Friedman of his meeting several days before with the great poet T. S. Eliot in London. They had been brought together by Ronald Gregor Smith, translator of *I and Thou* (still the best translation despite Walter Kaufmann's later one) and *Between Man and Man*. When Friedman asked Buber whether he did not find his own opinions different from those of Eliot, Buber replied: "When I meet a person I am not concerned with opinions but with the person." Friedman rightly took this response as a reproach because, as he later realized, he had turned Buber and Eliot into positions in a dialectic within his own mind and lost their reality as dialogical persons.

Springing from Friedman's relation with Buber, beginning in the summer of 1950 and ending with Buber's death in 1965, this work takes us from Friedman's earliest contact with Buber, through Buber's three visits to America, his wife's death, Friedman's stay in Jerusalem, and the articulation of Buber's culminating philosophy of the interhuman. To trace this chronology, Friedman draws extensively—particularly in chapters between Buber's visits to America—on his personal collection of letters between Buber and himself. These letters preserve the substance of their dialogue, bringing into focus subjects of mutual interest and opening a window on Friedman and Buber's shared intellectual concerns. The chapters drawn primarily from Friedman's fifteen years of correspondence with Buber retain the form of dialogue that was close to Buber's heart. Indeed, this book discloses Friedman's double dialogue with Buber—with his writings and with him personally—occurring on the "narrow ridge" between the either-ors of love and justice, dependence and freedom, the love of God and the fear of God, passion and direction, good and evil, unity and duality.

Friedman has organized these chapters chronologically according to the dialogical nature of their relationship. The narrative contains a dynamic network of stories in which a cast of prominent characters are introduced (e.g., Reinhold Niebuhr, Joseph Campbell, Will Herberg, Paul Tillich, Albert Einstein, Niels

Bohr, D. T. Suzuki, Abraham Joshua Heschel, and Carl Rogers), along with confessional reflections and Buber's personal and professional advice to Friedman. It was only shortly after their relationship started (which was due largely to Friedman's mother) that Buber surprised Friedman by suggesting that he translate Buber's essay "On the Suspension of the Ethical." Friedman resisted, saying, "I've never had a formal course in German." Buber responded, "I can tell you are faithful and you are readable." Thus began years of perhaps a dozen translations of Buber's books by Friedman always occurring in an ongoing dialogue with Buber in which Buber almost invariably had the last word. When Friedman requested Buber's personal advice about observing Jewish ritual and law, Buber answered from his own experience: "Put yourself in relation as you can and when you can, do your best to persevere in relation, and do not be afraid!" At the same time, in Buber's letter recommending Friedman for a position at Columbia University, he identified Friedman's "best quality" as understanding the ideas he met, even the person who thought them, and his "best faculty" as the ability to express and explain what he has understood.

Readers will notice, as well, Buber's personal character suffusing this book through details—known only to Friedman—that help to illuminate certain passages in his writings. In one of the seven seminars on the unconscious that Buber conducted for the Washington School of Psychiatry in 1957, Buber commented, "My friend Maurice Friedman knows more about me than I do." When Friedman asked Buber to write a foreword to his *Martin Buber: The Life of Dialogue*, Buber responded by asking, "Will you know what I mean when I tell you that I am not interested in myself?" *My Friendship with Martin Buber* thus is not a biography of Buber, but a remarkable account of sacramental dialogue (in Buber's terms) between person and person. Friedman's book allows us to get a sense of Buber as a person and not just as a famous author.

While Friedman originally wanted to call this book *All Real Living Is Meeting*, the central statement of Buber's great classic *I and Thou* (1923), the title that he finally settled upon—*My Friendship with Martin Buber*—reflects the fact that their relationship became the most meaningfully creative presence in Friedman's life. Indeed, Friedman continued to be in dialogue with and shaped by Buber's highly dialogic responses to his queries and concerns while they knew each other.[4] The importance of this book is reinforced by the German literary critic Grete Schaeder's observation that "Friedman has contributed more to the understanding of Buber in the United States than any other person."[5] According to Schaeder—who developed a close relationship with Buber between 1961 and 1965 while working on her comprehensive study (originally in German) *The Hebrew Humanism of Martin Buber* (1975)—when Buber read Friedman's doctoral dissertation on Buber, he was struck by its "thoroughness and its seriousness." In response, Buber sent Friedman all of his works that Friedman did not know. While Friedman was completing his book *Martin Buber: The Life of Dialogue* (1955), Buber patiently answered all of his questions, clarifying for Friedman many points of possible misunderstanding of Buber's work. Subsequently, Buber called *The Life of Dialogue*—now in its fourth English edition with new Appendices on Buber and Emmanuel Levinas and Buber and Mikhail Bakhtin—"the classic study of my thought," as he has done with no other work.

Friedman's first book on Buber gave rise to numerous other titles, including *Martin Buber and the Theater* (1969); the three-volume study *Martin Buber's Life and Work* (1981–1988), for which he did research for seven months in the Martin Buber Archives at the Jewish National and University Library at the Hebrew University of Jerusalem and which won the National Jewish Book Award for Biography from the Jewish Book Council in 1985; *Martin Buber and the Eternal* (1986); and *Encounter on the Narrow Ridge: A Life of Martin Buber* (1991), which was published in hardback and later in paperback in America, in two Spanish editions in Buenos Aires, in German translation, and in a Japanese translation in Tokyo. Along with translating into English, editing, and in many cases introducing many of Buber's books, Friedman has translated most of Buber's American lectures in *Eclipse of God* (1952), Buber's *Pointing the Way* (1957), and his *The Knowledge of Man: A Philosophy of the Interhuman* (1965). Adding *My Friendship with Martin Buber* to Friedman's already extensive body of work on Buber underscores the significance of Martin Marty's remark that "all subsequent work on Buber must build on Friedman's foundation." Because this book performs the kind of open, direct, mutual dialogue that Buber spent his life advocating, it is not difficult to envision Friedman's last—his most revealing—Buber book, *My Friendship with Martin Buber*, becoming essential reading, not only for Buber scholars, and scholars of Judaism, but also for those interested in American and Jewish intellectual history in the mid-twentieth century.

Acknowledgments

I should like to acknowledge with gratitude the work of James Brown.

By rearranging and tightening the manuscript, he molded a more consistent and readable text. James has provided decisive help with the demanding task of revision—of bringing the book into focus so that it might attain its true form.

I also wish to acknowledge with deep respect the contribution of my former student Kenneth Kramer, who has gone on to become a Buber scholar in his own right. He not only read various drafts of the manuscript—each time making valuable suggestions, including that I end it with my memorial address after Buber's death—but also was instrumental in bringing this book to publication by initiating contact with and handling all necessary correspondence between myself and Syracuse University Press.

Prologue

I was with Martin Buber in his three visits to America as well as during my four months with him in Jerusalem in 1960. My friendship with him begins in the summer of 1950 and ends with his death in 1965. The chapters that contain my selections from my fifteen years of correspondence with him retain the form of dialogue that was close to Buber's heart. I claim, nonetheless, that this book is more than just a personal memoir. It is a part of living history.

Although I never studied formally with Buber, he was, along with Abraham Joshua Heschel, my most important mentor. Through him I have come to a deep concern with Hasidism, biblical Judaism (the Hebrew Bible), psychotherapy, education, social philosophy and social problems, existentialism, and the life of dialogue—all of which I have given expression to in my books and my many articles.

Despite the disagreements in their interpretation of the prophets and of Hasidism, Heschel strongly protested Gershom Scholem's harsh critique of Buber's teaching of Hasidism. "Where do we have anyone else like him in world Judaism?" Heschel exclaimed to me. It is not surprising that Heschel, who happened to be in Jerusalem when Buber lay dying, tried repeatedly to get in to see him and that he often said to me that the man Buber was more important than his books!

I was able to sustain my simultaneous friendship and loyalty with Heschel and Buber for a great many years without feeling that I had to accept one and reject the other. This dual loyalty has meant living with the tension of the differences between the two men, such as their attitudes toward observance of the Jewish law. *My Friendship with Martin Buber* is composed of prose narration; of anecdotes from my personal contacts with Buber in his three visits to America and in the four months that my then wife Eugenia and I spent with him in Jerusalem, seeing him twice a week for long evenings; and several chapters of selections from Martin Buber's letters to me and my own letters to Buber. I want to give the reader a sense for both sides of the dialogue between Buber and myself. I hope that readers will find this exchange of letters rich and meaningful, as I do.

People often asked me if Buber really lived his philosophy. To this I can and will testify. He "walked his talk," as people like to say today. He really lived the life of dialogue, and to him it was really "the only life worth living," as Irving Howe, the editor of *Dissent*, said of Buber's friend Albert Camus.

Sixty years ago, my close friend Philip Griggs—who had brought me into his own dedication to Sri Ramakrishna and the Hindu Vedanta, who visited Swami Yatiswarananda with me once a week in Philadelphia, and who is now himself Swami Yogeshananda, director of the Atlanta Vedanta Center, wrote to me that I would one day find my guru. I have since left the path of the Vedanta. Nor have I ever related to any person as my guru in the traditional Hindu sense of the *chela*, following the guru with absolute obedience. But I have had the good fortune to have had an incomparable mentor in Martin Buber.

Despite my slight estrangement from Buber, much of which might be attributed to his age and ailing health, since Buber's death my loyalty to him has continued through countless lectures, seminars, and courses in this country and abroad. That this has included, on my part, some distancing from and contending with Buber has never dimmed my gratitude and love for Buber, both when he was alive and in the years since.

Maurice Friedman

Solana Beach, California

2009

My Friendship with

Martin Buber

1

My Friendship with Martin Buber Begins

Martin Buber's grandfather Solomon Buber was one of the great scholars and expositors in his day of the *aggadic* (nonlegal) portions of the Talmud. Although Martin Buber knew the Talmud, he did not draw heavily from those wellsprings. Martin Buber had a quality, which I inherited from him, of deeply caring about responding to one's unique personal call with a wholeness of the being that includes genuine decision and what the Hasidim called *kavana*—deep inner intention. Buber gave magnificent expression to this concern in his philosophy of dialogue for which he is known the world over, particularly through its classic formulation in *I and Thou*.

Buber had a lifelong devotion to gathering and retelling Hasidic tales, most of which were transmitted orally from generation to generation. The tales were not written down until a half century after the original transmission, when European Jews were afraid of losing them. To Buber, these tales, and not formal kabbalistic theories such as those of the Lurianic Kabbalah on which so much of formal Hasidic doctrines are based, were the real heart of the Hasidic community. Abraham Joshua Heschel once said to me that he saw Buber as an exception in that he mastered two fields—studies of the Hebrew Bible and of Hasidism—whereas most scholars of Judaism can master only one.

1

I was with Martin Buber during his three visits to America and I spent four months with him in Jerusalem in 1960. My friendship with him began in the summer of 1950 and ended with his death in 1965. Although I never studied formally with Buber, he was, along with Heschel, my most important mentor. Through him, I have come to a deep concern with Hasidism, biblical Judaism (the Hebrew Bible), psychotherapy, education, social philosophy and social problems, existentialism, and the life of dialogue—all of which I have given expression to in my books and nearly two hundred articles.

I was brought up as a Reform Jew, but Reform Judaism had little hold on me emotionally or intellectually. During high school and college, my ideals centered on peace and social reform. After college, during World War II, I spent three years in camps and units for conscientious objectors, and it was during that time that I realized the inadequacy of my social idealism. I discovered that though I wanted to help others, my own life had neither meaning nor wholeness. I became deeply interested in mysticism at this time, and through mysticism I found a belief in God and a meaning for my own life, but not for a religious way of life that seemed right for me. Vedanta appealed to me intellectually and Christianity emotionally, but I was not able to make either of these religions my own.

I grew up in Tulsa, Oklahoma, a pleasant and not too provincial southwestern city with a population at the time of 150,000. My parents both came from Europe: my father was from a *Mitnagdic* family in Poland and my mother from a Hasidic family in Lithuania. According to my great uncles, both of my maternal great-grandfathers belonged to the Lubavitcher dynasty. My mother's father spent most of his time in prayer and study, leaving the support and care of his family to his wife. I believe that it was partially in reaction to this that my mother turned to Reform Judaism, Zionism, and active organizational work of other sorts.

My home life was a chaotic and unhappy one. My mother dominated the family while my father largely withdrew from responsibility for the children. My mother was highly excitable and emotional as I grew up, and there were daily violent quarrels between my mother and father or some other member of the family (mostly me) that left me little inner peace. In my fights with my two-years-older sister Roberta, my mother usually sided with Roberta without asking any questions. I would mock or laugh at my mother when she got angry with me, which would infuriate her to the point that she would strike me with brooms, slippers, or anything else that came to hand. Before I was nine, I used to cry because my feelings were hurt, but after that I never cried.

In high school, I tended to draw back from my mother's attempts to press me forward or, in contradiction to her earlier treatment, to boast of my exploits. I had some good friends before I met Sarah Baker, a member of my classes all through high school who became my first emotional confidante. My relation with her was the deepest, most lasting, and significant one I knew for a number of years. I felt that Sarah and I understood each other at the deepest possible level and that we had an understanding that went beyond a particular knowledge of the other's qualities to an appreciation of the real essence of the other's being. For a while, Sarah was dependent on me, but by the end of high school the situation was reversed, and I found myself drawn to her by an emotional need that gave her a considerable advantage over me.

At Harvard in my junior year I studied the economics of Socialism and found myself at the end of college something of an unorthodox Marxist pacifist. While at college, my relationship with Al, a young Jewish girl from New York City whom I met in a summer work camp, led me to dedicate myself to the labor movement, and much of my work in that direction was colored by the rich emotions that I associated with her. The intellectual atmosphere of my group at Harvard was one marked by

pseudoscientific materialism and skepticism. We were dilettant-
ish and, we thought, sophisticated, prematurely "cynical," and
"futilitarian." While at Harvard, I heard Hans Kohn lecture on his
historical specialty, nationalism, but I did not know that he was
the author of the first comprehensive biography of Martin Buber,
published in 1930 long before he came to America. In fact, neither
I nor any of my intellectual Harvard friends had ever heard of
Martin Buber.

The question of pacifism weighed very heavily upon me
during my last years of college. My strong feelings about social
reform, international organization, labor, and Socialism had given
me an intense hatred and fear of fascism and Nazism, and I felt
very strongly about the Nazi treatment of the Jews. Yet since early
in high school I had regarded war as the greatest possible evil
and could not bring myself to support war even for the sake of
internationalism and social reform. I arrived at these convictions
through an intense inner struggle. I felt that never again in my life
would I have to make a decision as important as whether or not
to fight in World War II, and I sometimes felt that I would prefer
suicide to making the wrong choice. Though I did not believe that
war would accomplish anything, I was very much depressed at
being forced into inactivity. I knew in advance that the work in
the Civilian Public Service (CPS) camps to which conscientious
objectors were sent was mostly "made" work, that there was neither pay nor support in return for our work, and that the whole
atmosphere was one of compulsion.

Regardless, I spent three and a half years in Civilian Public Service camps for conscientious objectors from 1942 to 1946.
The camps I worked in were all run by the American Friends
Service Committee. In my first camp in West Campton, New
Hampshire, where I worked in the White Mountains felling trees
partially blown down by the 1938 hurricane, I began the practice
of meditation under the influence of Douglas Steere, a leading

Eastern Quaker in the United States. Steere introduced us to Soren Kierkegaard's beautiful devotional book, *Purity of Heart Is to Will One Thing*, and encouraged us to meditate, even if only for a few minutes every morning.

Civilian Public Service had a disintegrating effect on my personality, and no doubt that was true of others, too. In contrast to prisoners of war who were paid for their work, we really were slave labor. I believe that what finally gave me the positive emotional feeling that enabled me to make and carry out my decision to enter public service instead of fighting in the war was a growing belief in the power of passive resistance and in pacifism as a way of life. This combined with my Socialism to make me believe that the only true and effective revolution would be a nonviolent one. Although I did not believe nonviolence easy or even broadly probable, I believed it was the only effective way to combat fascism and to produce social reform. I felt that Nazism depended upon the negative consent of the governed and was unstable economically. On the other hand, I felt that war, instead of destroying fascism, would tend to produce it.

I carried my early practice of meditation over into my next CPS camp at Coleville, California, and the side or spike camps radiating out from it. One of my fellow campers, Henry LeRoy Finch, became alarmed at my steady movement toward mysticism. He had majored in philosophy at Yale whereas I had majored in economics, getting a magna cum laude in labor economics when I graduated from Harvard. At that time, I was a Socialist, aiming to become a labor educator, worlds removed from both religion in general and mysticism in particular. I had taken two courses in philosophy at Harvard, but these only introduced me to Plato, Aristotle, Descartes, Spinoza, and Leibniz. Roy opened the door for me to exciting contemporary thinkers such as Henri Bergson and Nicholas Berdyaev. But the most important thing he did for me was to suggest that I read Martin Buber, who combined mysticism and social action, in the hope that my movement toward mysticism would not lead me to altogether abandon social action with which he was very much concerned.

I remembered Roy's suggestion, but I did not act on his advice until a year and a half later. By that time I was an attendant at an institution for the "feeble minded," as the developmentally disabled were called at that time. More importantly, through my association with a *Gemeinde* of three other like-minded conscientious objector (CO) attendants, I had become a confirmed and thoroughgoing mystic through my reading of devotional literature of Christian, Hindu, and Buddhist mystics; three hours of meditation a day; and the repetition to myself of *mantras*, or Hindu song-words, when I was at work. I went every week to meet with Swami Yatiswarananda in Philadelphia, the local representative of the Ramakrishna-Vivekananda Order of India. I was exclusively concerned with an individualistic relationship to the Absolute and not at all concerned with forms of mysticism with a more social focus.

In my CPS camp in California, heat, fatigue, and restlessness made it more and more difficult to get through each day. Time seemed to stand still, and instead of being able to think with pleasure about what I had learned at Harvard, my mind wandered on its own until I felt at times that I could not bear it any more. Despite my desire to work hard, I could not do so, and I found myself increasingly demoralized at the end of each day so that nothing I did in the evening could restore a feeling of satisfaction. After two months at this camp, I went into the kitchen, where I found cooking truly creative. I became much happier, but I did not succeed in establishing good relations with other camp members, and I tended to come into conflict with both campers and foremen.

Out under the stars in Dog Valley, I began to realize that I had not yet come to terms with the meaning of life for myself and that trying to be of service to others before I had found either meaning or wholeness in my own life was an evasion. As a result, I rejected Marxian Socialism because it emphasized class conflict rather than the change in individuals from egoism to cooperation, which I saw as the real key to Socialism. I realized that I would have to change my own character before I could change others.

In the Institute for the Feeble Minded, where I worked as an attendant for a year and a half, I began regular periods of meditation of an hour two or three times a day. I believe it was only these periods of meditation that gave me enough peace and strength to meet the problems with which I was constantly confronted in my duties in the wards. Increasingly convinced of the value of an absolute pacifist way of life, I refused after the first few weeks to copy the regular attendants and my fellow COs in using a strap, a stick, or other methods of force to keep the patients in order. I gave up eating meat and in general restricted my diet as much as possible. I turned away entirely from an interest in girls and decided that my commitment to the spirit necessitated my leading a celibate life in some type of free monastic community. My efforts to combat pride and greed were considerably helped by regular devotional reading with our *Gemeinde* of four and by group and individual meditation.

Because of the demands of my mystical way of life, I cut myself off almost entirely from the regular life of the unit. I would never play cards, dance, or even, if I could help it, converse with the other members. I tried to feel the presence of God at every moment by means of silence, inner concentration, and the constant repetition of phrases from our then spiritual guide Brother Lawrence. My meditation greatly increased my sensitivity and often left me with a "caught" feeling in which my energy seemed suspended and not fully under my own control. Moreover, my constant efforts to suppress all aggression in favor of the love of God brought me into conflict with those with whom I worked. The sense of resignation and love that I sought was partly replaced with a desire for spiritual experiences and spiritual power. My periods of meditation no longer seemed to lift me into the timeless, and my efforts to concentrate resulted in tension in my eyes, my chest, and the back of my neck that stayed with me for months.

Home in Tulsa on a rare furlough, I told my mother enough about my interest in Hindu, Christian, and Buddhist mysticism that she became concerned. She told me something she had never even mentioned before—that her father in the Old Country (Russia at that time but earlier and later Lithuania) had been a devoted Lubavitcher Hasid. Despite my being a star Sunday School pupil in our Reform Jewish temple in Tulsa, I had never heard of Hasidism before or of the great impact it had on the Jews of Eastern Europe. Hasidism had been regarded as too obscurantist and irrational for the Reform Judaism of my youth. My mother asked me to talk with a local Conservative rabbi who sent me in turn to see his professor, Simon Greenberg, in Philadelphia. Rabbi Greenberg lent me Buber's early rendition of the legends of the Baal Shem (the eighteenth-century founder of Hasidism) plus *I and Thou*, Martin Buber's central philosophical work. These were the two primary volumes of Buber's works that had been translated into English at that time.

I had been sufficiently impressed by what Roy Finch had told me about Martin Buber during my mystical phase at the Coleville Camp that I was quite open to the loan of these two books. Greenberg was a distinguished Philadelphia rabbi and professor at the Jewish Theological Seminary in New York. I used to go see Rabbi Greenberg fairly regularly. Once, while having dinner at his home in Philadelphia, I met his elder son Moshe who already in high school was translating Shakespeare into Hebrew. Today, Moshe Greenberg is a distinguished professor of the Hebrew Bible (the so-called Old Testament) at the Hebrew University in Jerusalem. I have had contact with him over the years, and we met at two theological conversations in the Laurentian Mountains north of Montreal in Canada and in Jerusalem where I saw him on my last trip there in 1993. These two theological conversations, organized by Rabbi David Hartmann of Montreal, for many years now director of the highly original Hartmann Center in Jerusalem, were taken part in by Jewish scholars of every persuasion, including myself who was not a rabbi, and who belonged to no congregation; distinguished Reform rabbis and professors such as Eugene Borowitz and Emil Fackenheim; Conservative rabbis and authors such as Samuel H. Dresner; and the son-in-law of the great Orthodox rabbi and scholar Joseph Soloveitchik. It was in Montreal that I first met Elie Wiesel in 1964 or 1965.

My last period in Civilian Public Service was at a camp in Gatlinburg, Tennessee, and a spike camp in Smokemont, North Carolina. It was at this time that I read Martin Buber's *The Legend of the Baal-Shem* and *I and Thou* in good earnest. In the former, I found a religious tradition with which I felt in the closest sympathy, even though I had no immediate links with it. In the latter, I found a philosophy that expressed the meaning of life for me better than anything I had ever read. At the same time, through experiences in my own life I came to the conviction that my own way must lie in action and community rather than asceticism and contemplation. Despite my feeling for Hasidism, I felt that I could not honestly accept the rituals and observances of traditional Judaism. I was told and believed that I could not be a Hasid unless I was an observant Jew. I have since learned to read biblical Hebrew, though not fluently, and I have read a good deal about Judaism, Hasidism, and the Kabbalah. I have come to realize that I shall never be an observant Jew, nor can I revive Hasidism, as I once naively imagined. I wanted to learn to read Hebrew mainly that I might read Hasidism in the original texts, but I shall never make the study of Hebrew my lifework, as Gershom Scholem urged me to do when he talked to me at the University of Chicago where he came to visit my teacher Joachim Wach whom he knew in Germany.

In the spike camp in Smokemont, North Carolina, a group of COs set up a retreat on the weekends that some of us from different detached-service units attended. One camper sought to convert me to a monastic discipline that did not fit in at all with why I had come to this "retreat," and this inevitably led to conflict. Partly as an escape from this conflict, I spent what few furloughs I could get visiting a Harvard friend and his wife in nearby Chapel Hill, North Carolina, where I found that they were involved in an amateur psychodrama group. Ellie, the leader of this group, could not trust the process enough to relax her conscious control. She was the person who had the greatest and most difficult problems to resolve and around whom the group revolved. That some very remarkable things did happen—actions from out of the unconscious, unusual coincidences, understandings of all the members without the need of sign or speech, and at times deep feelings of being caught up in a process that was greater than the individuals involved—I can personally attest. At the same time, it eventually became clear to me that the group was undertaking a very dangerous thing. From a psychological point of view, the group was playing with fire—stirring up the unconscious without adequate enclosure or professional help or control. From the religious and moral point of view, much of the group's actions bordered on a daemonic desire for power and self-assertion—what Buber so aptly called "the lust for overrunning reality."

When I left my "psychodrama" friends, I was considerably confused as to what I now thought, but it was clear that I had been suppressing a great deal in my meditation and concentration and had been harming myself thereby. It was also clear to me that my emotions were too strong for the sort of emotionless calm that I had been trying to cultivate in Buddhism and Vedanta. The cosmos of Gerald Heard and Aldous Huxley that had given me security now fell to pieces, beyond hope of repair. It seemed clear to me that Heard's teachings were dangerous because they encouraged one to meditate on good and suppress the "evil"—the Hasidim would say the "evil urge"—-which was one of one's basic energies. I felt finally that in discovering the deeper emotions that I had suppressed I also had discovered my essential Judaism.

Freed from the conscription of Civilian Public Service in the spring of 1946, I began a master's program in English at Ohio State University in the fall and a year later entered, with a fellowship, the doctoral program of the Committee on the History of Culture at the University of Chicago. I had included Martin Buber's Hasidic chronicle novel *For the Sake of Heaven* in my master's thesis, *The Search for Faith in Ten European Novels*. Despite the fact that my master's degree was from the Department of English at Ohio, not one of these novels was originally in British or American English.

In my doctoral program at the University of Chicago, I focused on the comparative history of religion under the great scholar Joachim Wach, with a minor emphasis on Judaism and Jewish history and on the cultural history of Europe from the eighteenth to the twentieth centuries. My doctoral dissertation was titled "Martin Buber—Mystic, Existentialist, Social Philosopher: A Study in the Redemption of Evil." It was almost 600 pages long. At that time, Buber was practically unknown in America.

From the beginning of my graduate work, I found myself antagonistic to both research divorced from purpose and analytical thought divorced from emotion and intuition. The ideal of scholarship that I held before myself was that of "integral thought"—the integral combination of thought, intuition, and emotion. For this reason, I could not happily confine myself to philosophy abstracted from the concrete experience of literature and history. Nor could I study literature as meaningful in itself without reference to its relation to life and the search for meaning in life. The main defects in my teaching at the college of the University of Chicago while getting my doctorate were an undue allusiveness and complexity and an occasional tendency to inject too much humor or energy into the discussion that affected adversely the unity and purposiveness of the group.

Arnold Bergstrasser, the distinguished chair of my dissertation committee, once asked me if there was anything that would keep me from reading my dissertation ten years hence, wondering if I would really understand it at that later date. "Martin Buber has done so much work," he said, but "Martin Buber's secret is prayer." I do not think Bergstrasser meant conventional prayer, but a type of presence that Buber brought to everything he did. The last time I saw Bergstrasser was in Munich, Germany, in June 1960 when we both attended a reception for Buber after Buber had delivered his City of Munich prize speech, "The Word That Is Spoken," which I later translated into English for inclusion in Martin Buber's final, mature formulation of his philosophical anthropology, *The Knowledge of Man.* Some years after I received my Ph.D., in 1950, Bergstrasser gave up his professorship at the University of Chicago in favor of a position at the University of Freiburg, where he introduced political science as a whole new academic discipline in Germany.

Abraham Joshua Heschel, who knew Buber from Germany (Buber gave Heschel his first job, Heschel once told me), had cautioned me not to try to contact Martin Buber since he was a very busy man. Up till now I had heeded Heschel's injunction. Buber did not know that I was writing a doctoral dissertation on him, nor had I sought Buber's aid at any point. I had never had a course in German but had passed the language test through reading on my own. This stood me in good stead for my dissertation since I had to translate from German quite a lot of never-before-translated materials. Finally, though, at the end of my unusually long and quite demanding dissertation, I decided to write Buber a letter about it to send with my mother who was on her way to the new state of Israel to look up long-lost cousins in Kibbutz Kinneret on the Galilee.

In my letter to Buber, I told him that "I have been constantly amazed by the way in which your writings have spoken to my condition and fit my thought," adding that "those works that I most value in addition to *I and Thou* are your Hasidic Tales, the essays in *Hasidism,* and *Between Man and Man,* your essay on 'The Faith of Judaism,' and *For the Sake of Heaven,* which I consider one of the greatest novels I have read." I told Buber that I had "taken up your complete works in my dissertation, and I have centered my treatment of them in your attitude toward evil—broadly defined to include your religious philosophy, your philosophical anthropology, and your socialism." In my dissertation, I set Buber's attitude toward evil in a typology, ranging from the monist (now I would say "nondualist"), who regards evil as unreal, to the dualist who regards it as absolute and independent. The middle position, in which I saw Buber's thought, is the recognition that evil does exist, coupled with the belief that evil is not absolute and can be redeemed. I analyzed this position in terms of both Hasidic thought and Buber's conception of I and Thou, and I tried to show the relation between the two. "My main concern," I wrote to Buber, "has been with the internal consistency of your thought rather than with its sources or similar trends in other thinkers."

"I am sending you this letter through my mother," I concluded. "She is traveling in Israel and wants to see and talk to you, which I strongly urged her to do. My mother comes from a Hasidic family in Lithuania and, though she left her family for America when she was thirteen, she has, I believe, retained something of the Hasidic spirit. It is only thus that I can explain the tremendous attraction that Hasidism has had for me since I read your book *The Legends of the Baal-Shem* in 1944."

In 1950 it took my mother eight hours by bus to get from Kibbutz Kinneret to Jerusalem, but she made the journey. She insisted on seeing Buber and managed a long talk with him alone. I never knew what my mother said to Buber about me, but it led Buber to write me even before he received my dissertation. He said that what my mother had told him about me had led him to want to help me. He thought he could help me best if I were to write him the story of my life. "No analyses, please," said Buber, who was not a friend of psychoanalysis, "but tell the story without holding back." He also told me to send him my dissertation after it was bound.

I must confess that it is only now, more than half a century later, that I have adequately recognized the lengths to which my mother went to fulfill the task that I had set her of personally delivering my letter to Buber.

A month or so after this, I sent Buber my doctoral dissertation bound in two volumes along with a twenty-three-page autobiography, from which the above brief story of my life until then was drawn. Buber's response to my second letter has been decisive for my whole life since then. "You have a delightful gift of narration," he wrote me, "but you only tell us of how you feel about those included in your life story. You do not make us see them in themselves." He also declared my dissertation the best presentation of his thought. He said that the problem of evil, around which I centered my dissertation, was not only one possible way of organizing his thought, but the very best way. He offered to help me with the book that I would write on him. Eventually, in fact, my dissertation served only as the opening part of this book. Buber sent me a long bibliography of writings on him and his thought, all of which I had been unaware of until then despite the University of Chicago's excellent library.

My response to his letter? I fell on my knees, thanked God, and vowed to live up to the task that the letter set for me. Even though by no means has my whole lifework been devoted to Martin Buber, I think that I have lived up to this vow ever since. It proved to be a far greater commitment than I could ever have imagined. "I do not know if I can adequately communicate to you how happy your comments made me," I soon replied, "except perhaps to tell you that it is one of the two or three finest things that ever happened to me." In response to my letter and our developing epistolary dialogue, Buber tried repeatedly but unsuccessfully to find a Hebrew or German publisher for my first book, *Martin Buber: The Life of Dialogue,* which he himself went over carefully as I was writing it, making many suggestions and corrections. To this extent, it was a joint product of both of us. He testified that it was "the classic study of my thought," as he did about no one else's book on him.

2

The Cost of My Commitment

I spoke in the last chapter of having no notion of what the commitment to Buber would entail. I shall in this chapter sacrifice chronology and offer a few vivid illustrations of the price I would have to pay to honor the vow I made to fulfill my commitment to work with Martin Buber after I received a wonderful letter about my doctoral dissertation.

The fall of 1951 was my first year of teaching at Sarah Lawrence College—a progressive women's college outside New York City that was also enormously demanding for the faculty. Hearing that I was working on what later became my first book, *Martin Buber: The Life of Dialogue* (a title that Buber himself liked very much), an economist colleague at Sarah Lawrence said to me, "If you can get a book written while teaching at Sarah Lawrence, please let me know!" She left the very next year to teach at MIT. I stayed on for fourteen years and did, in fact, succeed in completing many books (including a dozen books of Buber's that I translated from German to English, usually with an editor's introduction).

I doubt that Martin Buber ever really understood the burden that I placed on myself during those years. Buber himself took on unbelievable tasks during his many, many years of active work, not to mention carrying on an active correspondence with scholars, educators, political and social activists, and countless others who sought the advice and help of this world-famous man of goodwill.

But Buber never taught in an institution of higher learning such as Sarah Lawrence College. What made Sarah Lawrence so difficult a place to teach in was the fact that, in addition to regular class meetings, every teacher met with each student once a week individually. These meetings were really tutorials—not about the subject matter of the course but about the individual interests of the student. This study and research eventually resulted in a "contract"—a term taken from the North Shore Country Day School outside of Chicago. In contrast to the traditional "term paper," the contract need have little or nothing to do with the subject matter of the course. Nor did it have an important part to play in the grades that students received for these year-long courses since there were no grades, only paragraph-long evaluations. Neither were there any academic majors nor any across-the-board student requirements. There was, to be sure, an important committee of faculty that kept track of the student's overall progress and could decide when the student in question was no longer qualified to remain in the college.

I often felt as if I were throwing out planks as far as my knowledge extended and then inviting the students to go out on the plank beyond my own knowledge! I seldom walked to a class without some student at my elbow discussing her present or future contract.

One other thing that made the Sarah Lawrence system more difficult for the faculty than any I have encountered before or since was the fact that the faculty also acted as "dons" for those of the students who chose this or that faculty as a don. Although the term "don" was borrowed from the universities of Oxford and Cambridge in England, that is where the resemblance ended. The British don is strictly a tutor whereas the Sarah Lawrence don is the overall student adviser. Again, though, this bore little or no relation to the general academic adviser that in most colleges or universities the students see about once a semester. When I first came to teach at Sarah Lawrence, the faculty met with the "donnees" every week, later every other week, but always with a total responsibility for every aspect of the student's life. This included whether she was spending too many weekends with her boyfriend at Yale, Harvard, Princeton, or Columbia.

Although the don-donnee relationship was not thought of as a form of therapy, it was at times the don's responsibility to refer the student to the college therapist if that seemed called for. (I discovered in practice that this transfer was not always easily made, since my donnee had built up a relationship of trust with me which she did not have with the unknown professional to whom I sent her—a psychological authority who might eventually recommend that her relationship with the college be terminated, as I could not and would not do!)

When the *Harvard Crimson* came to do a study of Sarah Lawrence, it featured me as the faculty member who made a "religion" out of the college. While this characterization was not entirely fair, neither was it entirely unfair. Before accepting the appointment, I read all the books about Sarah Lawrence that I could find; bought into the system lock, stock, and barrel insofar as I could understand it; and began my teaching duties with boundless enthusiasm and idealism.

Nor did fourteen years of teaching there help me to learn my limits. I used to have lunch with students so often to make up missed conferences that I felt as if I was not socializing with my colleagues. I admired Buber for his ability to say "no" as well as "yes" but had a hard time learning to do the same. Before I left the college, my courses became more and more popular. I sometimes had as many as twenty-five donnees at the same time!

I also had a fierce personal loyalty to my donnees. Once at a meeting at the home of the then dean—one of the founders of the college who later became president—I was appalled to hear all these powerful women speak as if the don owed exactly the same responsibility to all donnees, whether they were students he knew from the past or had just met!

I told the group of dons how that morning a student from one of my classes had come to me weeping because her room-mate and dear friend had been killed crossing the street from Kober House—a small off-campus house—to the main campus. Then I told the group of how another student, whom I had just met in class, had called me up that afternoon weeping and ask-ing if I would be her don. Since she too was from Kober House, I assumed that the reason for her weeping as she talked on the phone was because of the death that morning of her housemate and possibly friend.

Yet I asserted that my responsibility to the former student was greater than to the latter because the former had been my donnee the whole previous year and I had a personal relationship to her! I was struck by the fact that the powerful women at the meeting roundly attacked me whereas the men defended me. I remained the don of the latter student for the next three years and had a fine personal relationship with her.

Since this is something of a personal account, it may not be out of place to mention that the first student was Jane Quigley, later Jane Alexander, who became a great actress of stage and screen and was for four years director of the National Endow-ment for the Arts. I have been fortunate enough to stay in some contact with her over the years, the foundation of which is not only my great admiration for her as a professional and a person but also our close don-donnee relationship while she was at Sarah Lawrence.

I have often thought of writing a memoir subtitled "Mem-oirs of a Chocolate Mystic"—a name that my first wife Eugenia once dubbed me. Whether I am still anything of a mystic is in question, but I am certainly a "chocoholic"! Once in a one-on-one conference when Jane was my freshman donnee, she told me that there were two types of people—chocolate and vanilla. Vanilla people were superior to chocolate people, and she herself was a vanilla person. Although I have retained my love of chocolate, I have never had a problem in admitting her superiority. When she came to lecture at the University of California at San Diego, I reminded her of her vanilla-chocolate pronouncement, which she had totally forgotten. Jane was so amused by this that she signed my copy of her book about her years as director of the National Endowment of the Arts as "The Vanilla Girl"!

Jonathan Hermann, professor of philosophy and religion at Georgia State University and author of *I and Tao*—a book based on Martin Buber's early rendition of the parables of the great Chinese sage Chuang-tzu—was so troubled by my translation of "The Teaching of the Tao," a central text of that book, that he persuaded his university to give him a grant to spend a week at my house in Solana Beach, California, going through my files to see if he could find Martin Buber's corrections to my translation of his "Teaching of the Tao." (My translations were always part of an ongoing dialogue with Martin Buber in which he almost invariably had the last word!)

When we finally located Buber's corrections in a safe-deposit box in our bank, I was dismayed to find that they had evidently arrived too late for Harper to include them in its edition of Buber's *Pointing the Way*. As a result, some terrible bloopers remained in the text, such as my translating *Morganland* as "the West" instead of "the East"!

Before we came on Buber's corrections, however, we went through iron filing cabinets that I had not looked through for many years. When we did that, I was even more dismayed to realize how much of Buber's work I had loaded on myself during the 1950s and 1960s! That did not stop even when I spent a semester as visiting professor of philosophy of religion at Hebrew Union

College–Jewish Institute of Religion in Cincinnati—the seminary that trains Reform rabbis.

The saddest chapter for me personally was the time when I stayed up all night proofreading *Martin Buber and the Theater*—a book that hardly saw the light of day.

We missed the train from Florence to Naples that was our connection for a nonstop flight to Copenhagen. As a result we had to stop over for two hours in the Zurich airport. Too sleepy to stay awake, I failed to monitor my two children who were playing and fighting in the elevator. I was startled awake by the terrible crying and screaming of my six-year-old daughter Dvora, whose toes on her right foot had got caught in the elevator. While they found a crowbar to try to free Dvora, I held her in my arms, and she said over and over, "I want to die!"

I shall never forget this event. It will remain as vivid and excruciatingly painful in my mind and memory until I myself die. Dvora lost two toes from her right foot. She somehow managed to live with this loss and has grown up a strong person. For me, however, the anguish remains, and it is connected forever with my belief that I sacrificed much of the human for my work on Buber!

3

On the Suspension
of the Ethical

In the fall of 1950, Buber suggested that I translate his essay "On the Suspension of the Ethical." I objected that I did not see myself as a translator and had never in fact had a formal course in German. "I can tell," he replied, "you are faithful and you are readable." Thus began years of my translation of Buber's works, and in two cases his responses to essays and questions of others, which in many cases I edited and introduced. I would send Buber my translation, and he would send back a detailed commentary wherever he had a question. "On the Suspension of the Ethical" is the first essay of Buber's that I translated. It is also the first essay that I translated for Buber's book *Eclipse of God: Studies in the Relation of Religion and Philosophy*. Like all the others, while starting from a scholarly standpoint, it ended with a fervent statement about our time.

To Kierkegaard's claim that the "knight of faith" must suspend the ordinary ethical in favor of the "absolute duty to the absolute," Buber posed the question in this essay: "Are you really addressed by the absolute or by one of its apes?" Although the voice of Moloch prefers a mighty roaring to the "voice of a thin silence," in our age it appears to be extremely difficult to distinguish the one from the other. In the past, images of the absolute, "partly pallid, partly crude, altogether false and yet true," gave men some help

22

against the apes of the absolute that bustle about on earth. But now that "God is dead," in Nietzsche's words, and the eyes of the spirit "can no longer catch a glimpse of the appearance of the absolute," false absolutes rule over the soul, and the suspension of the ethical fills the world in exaggerated form. Well-conditioned young souls sacrifice their personal integrity in order that equality or freedom or "the kingdom" may come. (In his final version of the draft, Buber removed a reference to the kingdom out of consideration for Christian theologians.) "In the realm of Moloch honest men lie and compassionate men torture. And they really and truly believe that brother-murder will prepare the way for brotherhood!"[1]

"My wife Eugenia and I were both very much struck by this essay," I wrote to Buber in November 1950, "by the subtle way in which it puts its finger on the concept and the motivation of Kierkegaard's *Fear and Trembling*, by the close and yet compelling intensity with which it builds up to the last paragraph. I read the essay many times in German before I started to translate, and every time I got to the last part I found myself as much moved as the first time I read it."

Eugenia suggested that this essay might indicate a new phase in Buber's thinking about God, away from the conception of a sort of personal God, in which Kierkegaard believed, who could tell Abraham to sacrifice his son. I thought that any conception of God as entirely impersonal would be foreign to Buber's belief in the "eternal Thou." At the same time, I did not believe that Buber thought of God as a person who would command Abraham to sacrifice Isaac in order to test him. As I imagined the biblical event, Abraham did indeed receive a call from God to renounce everything for God's sake, but it was only Abraham who interpreted this call as a command to physically sacrifice (rather than to spiritually renounce his attachment to) Isaac.

If this were so, what God demanded of Abraham concerned more Abraham's relation to God than that to Isaac and did not constitute a "suspension of the ethical" at all. Even if Abraham was God's "chosen one," the chosen one is one who opens himself more fully to God than any other and is able to receive and accept to the fullest the demand that God puts upon his life. I did not conceive of this demand as something that God puts in terms of words or as something that could lead to the murder of one he loves.

Buber wrote to me, "I have not and I will never affirm a God who is simply impersonal." This was not an either/or question for Buber. He held that God is not a person but becomes one, so to speak, however contradictory the conception of God as both absolute and a person may appear. To Buber, God as "absolute Person" is not limited by other persons as we are, but needs us in order to know and be known, to love and be loved. The rationale underlying this is that we can only enter I-Thou relationships as whole persons, whereas the I-It relation is always only entered as a part of a person. Therefore, we must be whole persons to have an I-Thou relationship with God, which is the only relationship we can have with God because God can never become an It. Buber never spoke of God's essence, which we cannot know, not even in the language of metaphysicians and theologians, but only of our relationship with God as the "eternal Thou."

In the Postscript to the 1958 second edition of *I and Thou*, which Buber wrote in response to questions about *I and Thou* that he asked me to draw up for him, Buber expressed this notion of God as "absolute Person" with great clarity:

> The description of God as a Person is indispensable for every-one . . . who means by God, as I do, him who—whatever else he may be—enters into a direct relation with us men in creative, revealing and redeeming acts, and thus makes it possible for us to enter into a direct relation with him. This ground and mean-ing of our existence constitutes a mutuality arising again and again, such as can subsist only between persons. The concept

of personal being is indeed incapable of declaring what God's essential being is, but it is both permitted and necessary to say that God is *also* a Person. . . .

It is indeed the property of a person that its independence should consist in itself but that it is limited by the plurality of other independent entities, and this cannot of course be true of God. This proposition is countered by the description of God as the absolute Person, i.e., the Person who cannot be limited.

It is as the absolute Person that God enters into direct relation with us.[2]

As a Person, God gives personal life; he makes us as persons become capable of meeting with him and with one another. But no limitation can come upon him as the absolute Person, either from us or from our relations with one another; in fact, we can dedicate to him not merely our persons but our relations with one another. The man who turns to him, therefore, need not turn away from any other I-Thou relation, but he properly brings them to him and lets them be fulfilled "in the face of God."

One must, however, take care not to understand this conversation with God—Buber would have preferred the word "dialogue"—as happening solely alongside or above the everyday. God's speech to men penetrates what happens to each one of us, and all that happens in the world around us, biographical and historical. This turns it for you and me into instruction, message, and demand. Happening upon happening, situation upon situation are enabled and empowered by the personal speech of God to demand of man that he take his stand and make his decision. Buber said, "Often enough we think that there is nothing to hear, but long before that we have ourselves put wax in our ears."[3]

When the great German-American theologian Paul Tillich gave a farewell address to Buber at the meeting celebrating his going—the meeting at which Buber himself gave the important speech titled "Hope for This Hour"—he did Buber a great honor, particularly for the concept of God as "eternal Thou" by which he himself was decisively influenced. But he also remarked that his thinking was more Greek and Buber's more biblical, in the sense of being Hebraic. If he had been able to accept Buber's paradoxical description of God as the "absolute Person," he would not have had to speak of the "God beyond God"—the impersonal Godhead that cannot be addressed as Thou—at the end of his book *The Courage to Be*. Tillich's central insight in this book is his grasp of the courage to be in the face of the threat of non-being, and this is indeed a powerful insight. In Part One of my unpublished book *Foundations of True Community*, however, I speak of "the courage to address and the courage to respond," which I consider a great deal more existential and concrete than the "courage to be."

Professor Edward K. Kaplan of Brandeis University, author of a truly remarkable two-volume Heschel biography, once sent me a scholarly, informative, and in many respects invaluable article on Heschel and Buber that was published in 1994 with the generous inscription "To Maurice Friedman, with gratitude for your lifelong interpretation of Buber, In friendship, Ed." In this article, however, he made several statements about Buber's view of and relation to God that simply cannot stand. Heschel, Kaplan argued, [rejected] the reigning approach to culture and religion, characterized as "philosophical anthropology," which honored human vehicles (or "symbols") rather than the living God.[4] Briefly put, Buber, author of *I and Thou* (1923), inferred the existence of God from human encounters. Heschel would echo the unending voice from Sinai; he recognized that, despite his acute sensitivity to the inner life, Buber was an essentially secular thinker.

As Heschel said in an interview at the University of Notre Dame, "Reciprocity has two meanings: in relation to man and in relation to God. I am not sure that Buber used reciprocity in this second sense. In fact, I doubt it." However, in light of Buber's

Postscript to the second edition of *I and Thou*—not to mention Part Three of *I and Thou* proper, "Dialogue," his chapter "The Question to the Single One" in *Between Man and Man*, and his books *Moses, The Kingship of God, The Prophetic Faith, Two Types of Faith,* and *Israel and the World*—the statement by Heschel about Buber and reciprocity in his Notre Dame interview, the view that Buber was primarily a secular thinker, is patently absurd.

In my correspondence with Buber, I held that Kierkegaard was mistaken to base his "knight of faith" on the example of Isaac. Kierkegaard dealt with the temptation of Abraham throughout his *Fear and Trembling* as if Abraham had actually sacrificed Isaac and then had got him back rather than simply making ready to sacrifice him. This is shown most clearly by the parallel that Kierkegaard makes between Abraham's story and his own, in his infamous breaking off of his engagement with Regina Olsen. Kierkegaard does not say that the knight of faith should be prepared to sacrifice the princess and then desire to keep her. Instead, the knight of faith should be prepared to sacrifice the princess but should remain with her in a higher order, untroubled by jealousy and regret. Kierkegaard's entire interpretation of Abraham's sacrifice, I told Buber, justified Kierkegaard's failed relationship by allowing him to imagine an ideal person who would have carried it off with internal as well as external grace.

"On looking back at your essay, however," I wrote to Buber, "I doubt that you would agree with my symbolical interpretation of the event" because in Buber's words, "There is nothing to interpret here," since "the man who hears learns entirely what is demanded of him; the God who speaks proposes no riddles." "Also," I added, "when you say that he allows Abraham's readiness to grow to the full intention to act, he does not intend to allow Abraham to act 'unethically'" in his relation to Isaac. "He did intend for him to have to choose between his relation to Him (God) and his love for and desire to act ethically toward Isaac."

This reminded me of Buber's statement in his novel *For the Sake of Heaven*—that the gateway to God is dread—and his statement at the end of *Imitatio Dei* that the ultimate, secret working of God is terrible and does not stand with mercy and grace as attributes of God but stands somehow above them.

In response, Buber wrote to me, "The idea of an *entirely* impersonal God has no place in my thought, and will, I hope, never find one." When I expounded my reading of the story of Abraham's sacrifice to Buber in person a year later when he visited our home, however, he remarked simply, "There is not a word in the text that suggests that!"

In asking me to translate a second essay, "Religion and Reality," which expounded a thesis concerning the development of modern thought, Buber wrote that "I think [it has a] particular importance for our time." Tracing a thread of development through Spinoza, Kant, Hegel, Nietzsche, Bergson, and Heidegger, Buber characterized the thinking of our time as aiming to preserve the idea of the divine as the true concern of religion while destroying the reality of the idea of God and of our relation to him: "This is done in many ways, overtly and covertly, apodictically and hypothetically, in the language of metaphysics and of psychology," he said. Specifically, modern thought can no longer endure a God who is not confined to man's subjectivity. Wherever man has to interpret an encounter with God as a self-encounter, his very structure is destroyed. "This is the portent of the present hour," he wrote. Buber was particularly eloquent in his rejection of Bergson's conflating of God with a creative process:

> The divine force which man actually encounters in life does not hover above the demonic, but penetrates it. To confine God to a producing function is to remove Him from the world in which we live—a world filled with burning contradictions, and with yearning for salvation.[5] The modernist conception of God as a

creative, psychological force ended by "making the concept of God utterly meaningless."

In place of the "death of God," Buber described these conceptions of God as the "eclipse of God," a real happening that does not take place *in* God but *between* us and God. "Eclipse of the light of heaven, eclipse of God—such indeed is the character of the historic hour through which the world is passing," Buber wrote.[6] If one insists, like Heidegger, that it is within earthly thought that we discover the power that unveils the mystery, one denies the effective reality of our vis-à-vis and contributes to the human responsibility for this eclipse. We can do away with the name of God, which implies a possessive, but as Buber says, "He who is denoted by the name 'lives intact' in the light of His eternity. But we, 'the slayers,' remain dwellers in darkness, consigned to death."[7]

The two other essays that Buber sent me in August 1951 were "Religion and Philosophy" and "Religion and Ethics." "Religion and Philosophy," which contrasted philosophy as the bond between the absolute and the general with religion as the bond between the absolute and the Particular, was the hardest single piece of Buber's that I ever had to translate.

In the mail with those essays, Buber wrote me a long letter with thirty-one separate points answering questions I had put to him in connection with what later became my book *The Life of Dialogue*. He confirmed my perception that tragedy in *For the Sake of Heaven*, and the heart of tragedy in general, consists of two contending persons being each as he or she is without sufficient resources to bridge the opposition. "I was interested to see that you regard the situation in *For the Sake of Heaven* as one of tragedy rather than of good against evil," I wrote to Buber in 1951. I had thought in the past of tragedy along the Aristotelian lines I had learned in college, which emphasized the idea that tragedy consists not only of a downfall of the hero due to a defect but also a righting of the order of the universe through the voluntary suffering of the hero in atonement for his wrong. It seemed to me then that there was something about the nature of human personality that inevitably brought it into conflict with the order of the universe, and that there was a very real loss in terms of personal value through the suffering and perhaps death that Aristotelian tragedy assumed would reconcile man with the universal order. The classical Greek hero's acceptance of his responsibility not only for his conscious action but also, like Oedipus, for his unintentional ones constituted a real triumph of the human personality, I believed. I equated "personal" here with the acceptance of responsibility even beyond the demands of justice, and I contrasted this affirmation of the human personality with those men who do not relate to the universe as integral, responsible beings but rather as a collection of reactions to environmental stimuli, as determined beings.

My encounter with Buber's work got me to see that I was using the concepts "personality" and "responsibility" in a way that did not make sense. My Aristotelian sense of tragedy assumed that an individual's responsibility was not to another person or Person but to an impersonal order. "I also see clearly now," I wrote to Buber, "that the truly tragic in life" emerges not from "our inability to conform with or profit from the natural order" but from "our limited ability to give to each other in relationship, to remain open and to respond."

Once one recognizes that the two basic human attitudes "I-Thou" and "I-It" are probably mixed in each action, one is left with the tormenting doubt of whether in a particular action the "Thou" relation is sufficiently constant to permeate and enclose the "It" or whether the "I-Thou" attitude is only the thin front for motives that one would not like to admit to oneself. It is in this sense that I understood the despair that Kafka expressed in *The Castle*, in which there is a movement from the "Thou" to the

"It" even as there is a movement from the "It" to the "Thou." To believe in the redemption of evil means believing in the possibility of a movement from "It" to "Thou"; the permeation of the "It" is fundamental. This movement, and the responsibility it entails, corresponds to the oneness of the world with God—a oneness that is still to be accomplished yet is guaranteed by the oneness of God and his relation to men and to the world. The personal begins with this relationship; for in our human relationships we never know the pure "person" or pure "Thou," yet we always look for it and believe in it. God is the reality of the human "Thou," though God is never a universal essence.

The problem of evil enters in through the fact that we are not as interested in confirming as being confirmed, in making present as being made present. As a result of this self-centeredness, we limit our own confirmation by not confirming others. "Perhaps," I suggested to Buber, "this is what you meant in your essay 'Distance and Relation' when you wrote, 'That this capacity for confirmation lies so immeasurably fallow is the real weakness and questionableness of the human race.'"

Buber was concerned in his work that the movement from I-It to I-Thou not create another subject in the form of a Thou. In response to a question I put to him about Christian theologies that converted the I-Thou to a Thou-I, he wrote, "I am most decidedly opposed to the theologies putting the emphasis on the Thou as subject. They have not grasped the mystery of creation of man." This would also apply to similar "Thou-I" emphases in the Jewish theology of my late and dear friend Abraham Joshua Heschel. In this same letter Buber wrote: "Everything that I have written on dialogical existence means ontology—but not," he added, "ontological analysis." Buber was particularly concerned that I not mix his thought up with the existential philosophy of Martin Heidegger, who was gaining great prominence in German thought and for whose thought Buber did not care.

In opposition to Kierkegaard, who distinguished three quali-
tatively different stages in life's way—the aesthetic, the ethical,
and the religious—and made the choice between the aesthetic
and the ethical an absolute either/or, Buber wrote to me that

> aestheticism is degeneration, the aesthetic attitude is an indis-
> pensable part of true life, and the real aesthetic attitude is never
> autonomous. I had to overcome the aestheticism of my youth,
> but I do not remember in my life a conflict between the aesthetic
> and the ethical. (It must be noted, by the way, that Kierkeg-
> aard's misunderstanding of the category of the aesthetical has
> been fatal.)

Buber also held the I-Thou relationship with nature, from which
the West's Romantic aesthetic movement emerges, to be real but
not complete because it lacks genuine reciprocity. "The process
of self-becoming is important," he wrote me, "but it is necessary
to distinguish it from 'psychological egotism,'" of which he saw
Jung as an example. In fact, Buber hesitated to publish a new edition of his 1913 book *Ecstatic Confessions* because he believed, in
his later years, that it was "too mystical." A new edition of *Ecstatic
Confessions* was published after Buber's death.

Buber wished that I would bring out the epistemological consequences of his thought in *The Life of Dialogue*, which I did in
a separate chapter on Buber's theory of knowledge that the philosopher Emil Fackenheim singled out for special attention in an
article on Buber in *Commentary*. This epistemological thought,
he insisted, "must not be done by bringing my thought closer
to Heidegger to whom I am more opposed than ever although
I feel myself as in the days of my youth, and even more, near to
Heraclitus whom he treats as his father." "I think his interpretation of Heraclitus utterly erroneous," he added in parentheses.
In 1958 Buber wrote a major essay based on Heraclitus that was

published in 1965 in his book *The Knowledge of Man: A Philosophy of the Interhuman.*

Buber's advice to me as a biographer shortening my dissertation into a book was that I focus away from Buber himself and focus instead on what was "essential to the understanding of the ideas themselves; all the rest," he wrote, is less important." Advising me strongly that in my book I should avoid above all detailed exegeses of separate essays, he insisted that "if you have to sacrifice, sacrifice Buber." This was in keeping with the spirit of Buber's attitude toward his life as an object of student writing. When my old friend Arthur A. Cohen suggested to me that I ask Buber to write a Foreword to *The Life of Dialogue,* Buber responded by saying, "Will you know what I mean when I tell you that I am not interested in myself?" I never again raised the question with him.

Instead, I was becoming increasingly concerned about the implications of Buber's thought for concrete daily life, for the person confronted with psychological problems, for the person confronted with important personal and social problems, for the person who is trying to find a meaningful religious life in the modern world, and for the Jew who would like to evaluate Buber's interpretation of Hasidism and Judaism to aid himself in finding what in Judaism is essential for his way of life and what could or should be discarded.

One thing I had left over from my experience trying to follow a mystical way of life was a reluctance to speak of God in a direct and immediate way when I no longer felt the presence of God. When the enormous tensions that built up in work camps, in meditation, and in the experience of my psychodrama group began to dissipate, I began to feel that my religious way of life was slipping away and that my experiences of the presence of God were becoming more and more of a memory. What I now wanted was a way of life in the world and as part of a community, and I hoped to find that in Hasidism. I found in my readings in Hasidism a wonderful spirit and emotion, but I had not discovered how to make that spirit and emotion real in my own life. "I have always felt that if I talked with you," I told Buber, "you could help me with this problem and that perhaps no one else could. . . . In the last few months, I have begun to glimpse the possibility of a religious way of life that expresses itself in a tension held in daily living that enables one to meet what occurs in daily life and the problems of national and international conflict from a depth that gives this meeting 'religious seriousness' without divesting it of humor or flexibility and without any conscious 'practice of the presence of God' or mystical recollection."

In September 1951, I accepted a position at Sarah Lawrence College. In July of that year, Buber had written to let me know that he had read my translation of his "On the Suspension of the Ethical" on BBC Radio in London. "I hope to come to America at the end of October," he noted briefly. This news filled me with joy and some trepidation, for I had not yet met Buber, who was fast becoming more than a dissertation topic, but a teacher in the fullest sense, face to face.

4

Martin Buber's
First Visit to America

In November 1948 Louis Finkelstein, director of the Jewish Theological Seminary of America, an institution that trains Conservative rabbis, approached Buber about coming to America to lecture at the seminary. Buber responded warmly that he would like to meet the next Jewish generation face to face in the immediacy of life and not just through his books, for he was more than ever convinced of its significance "for our future." Because of his work in the Israeli School for the Education of Teachers of the People that he had founded and directed, Buber twice had to postpone coming, so that his first visit to America did not take place until the academic year 1951–1952. On October 31, 1951, Martin Buber flew with his wife Paula from Israel to New York. The Jewish Theological Seminary put them up at the Hotel Marcy on Ninety-sixth Street and West End Avenue in New York City.

Buber came to America for the first time to participate in a large lecture tour on both coasts, often appearing in colleges and universities but just as often outside. I remember vividly our first meeting face to face. Since I had seen his photograph with his great face and impressive beard so often, I was astonished by how short he was—just less than five feet tall. When we sat down at the Hotel Marcy, he commented on my mother's visit to him in Jerusalem. Then he told me of meeting the great poet T. S. Eliot in London during his five days' stay there just before he came to New York. T. S. Eliot was one of my all-time favorite poets, so this deeply interested me. Buber had been brought together with Eliot by Ronald Gregor Smith, who produced the first (and to my mind still the best) translation into English of *I and Thou* as well as *Between Man and Man* (the book of philosophical essays that followed *I and Thou*), which included Buber's first work devoted entirely to philosophical anthropology, his essay "What Is Man?" This last work was published separately in German in a smaller edition under the title *The Problem of Man*. Smith was professor of theology at the University of Glasgow. He had spent a week with Buber at his home in Germany before undertaking the translation of *Ich und Du*.

My love for Eliot's poetry was unmatched by my attraction to any other poet. Yet I had a problem with his neo-orthodox attitude toward evil. Eliot seemed not to espouse a full-scale dualism of good and evil, like many Gnostics and Manicheans, who held that evil is radically real and unredeemable. Eliot placed so much emphasis on evil that I could not see where he held humankind to be redeemable. When I met Buber, I had not yet read the writers who accused Eliot, not entirely unjustly, of anti-Semitism.

Buber told me that while Eliot was a shy man, he had a frankness that Buber really liked. I tried to draw him out further by asking him whether he did not find that his opinions differed from Eliot's in important respects. "When I meet a man," Buber replied, "I am not concerned about his opinions but about the man himself." I took this as a reproof, as indeed it was. In my mind, Buber and Eliot had stopped being real persons and had become chessmen in a dialectical game.

Since this was Martin Buber's first time in New York City, he was concerned to find an American publisher that would publish his books. Up to this point, not one translation of Buber's works had been published in America. I accompanied Buber to talk with the editors at Harper. In the course of our meeting, Buber spoke of what he saw as my "selfless" concern for his thought. From this time on, I became Buber's unofficial literary agent in America.

As he had been in postwar Europe, Buber was immensely popular in America, where he gave seventy-three lectures between 1951 and 1952. I do not believe that I am being immodest in suggesting that I played an important role in the upswing of Buber's thought and work in America. My translations and my book *Martin Buber: The Life of Dialogue*—which the great American theologian Reinhold Niebuhr said in the *New York Times Review of Books* was of "first importance for Jewish and Christian thinkers"—contributed to some extent to Buber's reception in the United States. Yet by the same token I was myself taken up in the upswing—no small part of which was carried forward and upward by European and European-American Protestant theologians, such as Karl Barth, Reinhold Niebuhr, his brother H. Richard Niebuhr, and Paul Tillich, upon whose thought Buber's had had a revolutionary effect, as I demonstrated at length in the "Buber and Christianity" chapter of *The Life of Dialogue*.

Buber made sure upon our first meeting to impress upon me that having a book about his thought written was less important to him than human relationship. "You must not think that I am interested in you only because you are writing a book on me," he stressed. "Books are not the most important things to me. They are just snakeskins that I shed as I go along."[1] A few days after my long conversation with Buber, I asked my wife Eugenia, who had not yet met him, to take to him my translation of a lecture that he needed for an out-of-town engagement since I was hopelessly tied up at Sarah Lawrence College. "Don't expect him to talk to you," I said to her. "He has only a half hour to make the plane to Cleveland." When Eugenia came in, Buber asked her to sit down. "What work do you do?" he asked. "I was a college teacher," she replied, "and I worked two years as a university librarian. Now I am trying to find a job as an editor." "Pardon me," said Buber and laughed, "but I don't see you at all as an editor. I see you rather as working with young children. But not boys over nine," he added. "Women cannot understand them." Buber's words came at the very moment of decision for Eugenia. She received two offers of editorial positions in the following weeks but turned them down in favor of getting a second master's in early childhood education (she already had one in English), which led to years of highly successful and rewarding work as a nursery school teacher.

Eugenia brought a rare presence to nursery school work that no training or techniques could have given her. When she asked Buber later how he knew with such sureness which path she should follow, he answered, "I do not know." He related to people not through techniques but through presence. I must add, however, that in the times Eugenia worked with me on my own writing over the years, she has proved herself an excellent editor. When Eugenia came home from her meeting with Buber, she discovered that I had a few days earlier already sent off for a catalogue from the Teachers College at Columbia because I was so struck by her response to her work at a preschool in Chicago the previous summer. Buber particularly appreciated Eugenia, he told me, "because she has the sort of active intelligence that I like."

Martin Buber's coming to America was also the occasion for his retirement from the Hebrew University of Jerusalem where he had taught since he had moved to Palestine in 1938. ("Palestine" did not become "Israel" till 1948.) Now that he had retired, Buber was asked to teach a seminar in biblical faith when he returned— a topic that had been strictly forbidden him as long as he was serving the university full time. "Why can I do it now when I could not then?" Buber complained to me. The answer, of course, was that opposition by Orthodox Jews had prevented his teaching religion in any official capacity in the university. Ultimately, after his return to Jerusalem, Buber was asked to teach a seminar in comparative religion, which he accepted.

I never took a note during or even after my many conversations with Buber, so what has remained of them is only what Buber himself called the work of the "organic selective memory." At his public lectures and in seminars and discussion groups, however, I did take notes. One of these discussion groups was a small group that met with Buber in his hotel suite at the Marcy. Buber did not lecture to us. He simply answered questions. Asked what proof he could give for his religious attitudes, he answered: "The 'man of faith' (I prefer not to say 'believing man') has decided for faith without objective proof and precisely this is his situation." Explaining his pedagogy in the context of his understanding of religion, Buber said in this meeting:

> What I mean by religion is just one's personal life. One usually does not dream of putting his personal life at stake—of really meeting abyss with abyss. I must, by violence of the spirit, bring the person I meet to deal with his personal life. I must not show him that his arguments are wrong by their content but that argumentation as such is wrong. I must break down his security by driving him to confront his self. He puts me in a situation of responsibility for him, struggling with him against him—using as allies the forces deep within him. It is just a question of personal relationship—nothing else.

One of those who made up this small group was Steven Hay, an ambivalent "disciple" of Buber's who had set out as a very young man to meet Gandhi but because of the assassination of Gandhi went instead to meet Martin Buber, who then sent him to meet me. Steven was the first one to ask a question at this particular meeting. "How do your books help people live their daily lives?" he asked, implying that they did not. "If you don't like my books, burn my books!" responded Buber without a trace of anger or irony.

Malcolm Diamond, later a professor of religion at Princeton University, who was writing a doctoral dissertation on Buber that became a book, raised the question of "subjectivity" in Buber's thought. "Subjectivity always means opinion, reflection," answered Buber. "I don't speak of this at all—only about being, existing." He was also not talking about "objectivity," he explained. "God has to do with every living being but not with ideas," he said. "Philosophical thinking is a transposition of reality to another plane altogether."

Perhaps the most important thing Buber said in his discussions regarded his relationship to Judaism. Asked about the Jewish law, or *Halakhah,* Buber conceded that his position might be mistaken for antinomianism or lawlessness, and that it might be used by an irresponsible person to confirm him in his irresponsibility. But for the responsible person, Buber saw the personal as the only way. "In three hundred years there may be a new *Halakhah,*" Buber said:

> But now this is just the way of the modern man. I am only against life becoming rigid. I want to warn man against anticipated objectification. Of course, objectification will come again and again, and when it does, the tradition can only be renewed through the personal way. On the personal way one may discover things that are not only true for oneself but for others. One cannot live without danger, without risk—the question is to choose between risks.

In no sense did Buber proceed as a theologian who accepts what the tradition says simply because it is the tradition. He would only affirm what he could confirm out of his own personal testing and wrestling. "There are things in the Jewish tradition I cannot accept at all," Buber told us, "and things I hold true that are not expressed in Judaism. But what I hold essential has been expressed more in biblical Judaism than anywhere else—in the biblical dialogue between man and God. In Hasidism," he continued, "this is developed in a communal life. I want to show that Judaism can be lived. It is most important that the Jews today live Judaism."

According to an itinerary Buber showed me shortly after his arrival, between early November and December 21 of 1951, he would deliver twenty lectures in New York, Cleveland, Chicago, and Detroit and at such colleges and universities as Dartmouth, Haverford, Brandeis, Yale, Columbia, the University of Chicago, and the University of Wisconsin. The three lectures that Buber gave for the Jewish Theological Seminary had to be moved from the Seminary to the Horace Mann Hall of Teachers College, Columbia, because of the great number of people who wanted to attend. In addition to these lectures, Buber received a stream of visitors, met with publishers, carried on an active correspondence with people around the world, worked with me on the translations of his lectures, and worked with Professor Seymour Siegel of the Jewish Theological Seminary on the pronunciation of his English. "Thou" was the one word Buber could never master. It always came out "vow."

By the time Buber came to lecture in America, I had moved from Ohio State University to Sarah Lawrence. By this happy synchronicity, I was able to attend many of Buber's lectures in New York City and make time to meet with him individually and sometimes with small groups. I had translated into English most of the essays in *Eclipse of God: Studies in the Relation between Religion and Philosophy*, which Buber used extensively in his lectures in America in the academic year 1951–1952. I passed out tickets to Buber's lectures to a number of my colleagues at Sarah Lawrence College, one of whom—the musicologist and composer Andre

Singer—spoke to me of his great gratitude to Buber for what his lectures had done for him when he lived in Vienna. During one of his Vienna lectures, Buber said:

> A home and the freedom to realize the principle of our being has been granted us anew, but Israel and the principle of its being have come apart. . . . People try to conceal the rift by applying basic religious terms, such as God of Israel and Messiah, to purely political processes . . . but the holy reality escapes any speech that does not mean just it, that is, the fulfillment of God's truth and justice on earth. True, it is a difficult, a tremendously difficult undertaking to drive the plowshare of the normative principle into the hard soil of political fact; but the right to lift a historical moment into the light of what is above history can be bought at no cheaper price.

During the discussion after this first lecture, a man said to Buber that he ought not despair so quickly about the State of Israel. "Despair!" exclaimed Buber. "I never despaired even in the darkest days of our people!"

In his second lecture, "The Silent Question," Buber presented Judaism through a critique of two modern Jewish thinkers who turned away from it—Henri Bergson and Simone Weil. Both Bergson and Weil saw Judaism as an embodiment of a principle of social life, which was either a stage to be surpassed, as for Bergson, or a terrible obstacle, the Great Beast of the Apocalypse, according to Weil. In opposition to the dualism both posited between that spiritual interior in which they found their touchstone of reality and the external social world, Buber held that while Judaism accorded inwardness a proper place, these writers overplayed the self-sufficiency of the soul: "Inward truth must become real life, otherwise it does not remain truth. A drop of Messianic consummation must be mingled with every hour; otherwise the hour is godless, despite all piety and devoutness." Social humanity built upon real relationships between its members was fundamentally different from Weil's "Great Beast," Buber argued. "Judaism rejects the 'We' of group egotism, of national conceit and party exclusiveness," Buber told his audience, "but it postulates that 'We' which arises from the real relationships of its components and which maintains genuine relations with other groups." Buber believed that he who loves brings God and the world together, and that this Hasidic teaching was the consummation of Judaism. It is realized, if anywhere, in the very kind of "active mysticism" for which Bergson called.

In an impassioned statement, Buber characterized the Hasidic message to all as "You yourself must begin":

> For the sake of this your beginning, God created the world. He has drawn it out of Himself so that you may bring it closer to Him. Meet the world with the fullness of your being and you shall meet Him. That He Himself accepts from your hands what you have to give to the world, is His Mercy. If you wish to believe, love!

In other words, existence will remain meaningless for you if you yourself do not penetrate into it with active love and if you do not in this way discover its meaning for yourself. Everything is waiting to be hallowed by you; it is waiting to be disclosed in its meaning and to be realized in it by you.

Buber's third seminary lecture, "The Dialogue between Heaven and Earth," uncovered the relationship between Buber's interpretation of the Hebrew Bible and his philosophy of religion with an explicitness that cannot be found in any of his other writings.[2] "The basic doctrine which fills the Hebrew Bible," Buber argued, "is that our life is a dialogue between the above and the below." To the sovereign address of God, the eternal Thou, man, even in his silence, offers his autonomous answer. In the acts of lamenting, supplicating, thanks- and praise-giving, man experiences himself as heard and understood, accepted and confirmed. Furthermore, "in the infinite language of events and situations, ever-changing but plain to the truly attentive, transcendence speaks to our hearts at the essential moments of personal life. And there is a language in which we can answer it—our actions and attitudes, our reactions and our abstentions." This understanding of the totality of our responses as our responsibility in the dialogue with transcendence is almost identical to what Buber wrote in 1957 in the Postscript to the second edition of *I and Thou* without referring at all to the Bible. Warning that we must be careful not to understand the conversation with God as something happening solely outside the everyday, Buber declared that "God's speech penetrates everything biographical and historical in our lives and makes it for you and me into instruction, message, demand." As he explained in his Postscript, "Happening upon happening, situation upon situation are enabled and empowered by the personal speech of God to demand of the human person that he takes his stand and make his decision."[3]

It is also in "The Dialogue between Heaven and Earth" that the real heart of Buber's understanding of this hour as one of the "eclipse of God" is laid bare. When God seems to withdraw himself utterly from the Earth and no longer participates in its existence, the space of history is full of noise but empty of the divine breath. "For one who believes in the living God, who knows about Him, and is fated to spend his life in a time of His hiddenness, it is very difficult to live." Indeed, Buber asked, "How is a Jewish life, or more correctly, a life with God still possible in a time in which there is an Auschwitz?" Elie Wiesel, himself a survivor of the Shoah, said, "With the advent of the Nazi regime in Germany humanity became witness to what Martin Buber would call an eclipse of God."[4] It was because of what I have called "the Job of

Auschwitz" that Buber called our postwar age that of "the eclipse of God." However, like the biblical Job taught, we do not "stand overcome before the hidden face of God" or "put up with earthly being." Instead, "we struggle for [Earth's] redemption, and struggling we appeal for the help of our Lord, who is again and still a hiding one."[5]

Referring to Buber's courage in the face of the Nazi regime, Abraham Joshua Heschel, who said that Buber the man was even greater than his books, spoke of activities in Nazi Germany as the time of his truest greatness. Buber's disciple Ernst Simon said that the greatest example of civil courage he knew was Buber giving a lecture in Berlin to a great many people, knowing that in the audience there were many SS men. Buber himself once said, suggesting the spirit of Job, "I do not understand how one can live at all without courage."

As Buber gave lectures in America, he was very much like a formal professor in Germany, but after his lectures, he always made a point of speaking person to person. After a lecture at Yale University, Buber spoke for twenty minutes with a woman who had asked him a question from the audience. Years later, she spoke of how much this dialogical immediacy had meant and still meant to her. Buber's immediacy in dialogue, however, was not always gratifying to others. Once before a dinner at Yale in his honor, when the host said, "Professor Buber will deliver grace," Buber said shortly, "Don't believe in it." Buber would not allow individuals who came to visit him personally to take notes, for his concern was with whole-person-to-person dialogue rather than with imparting information.

One of Buber's most remarkable lectures on his first visit to America took place at the Park Avenue Synagogue in New York City. There, he presented one of his interpretations of the Psalms from his small book *Right and Wrong*, later part of a larger existential exegesis. At one point, he said with all possible emphasis on the words of the Psalm, "I shall not die but live." It seemed the most personal declaration conceivable and at the same time a confession made for all Israel. After the lecture, Buber answered questions informally. Clearly implying that Buber was perhaps not the best Jew, one audience member asked, "Professor Buber, why have you had such an influence on the Protestants?" to which Buber responded, "Ask the Protestants!" Another attendee asked a question so forgettable that Buber had to ask, "Have you really lain awake at night thinking about this question?" In distinction from most lecturers, Buber never dealt with general cultural questions. In public settings he would only answer what he called "real questions," questions on which the questioner staked him- or herself. "This is really *pilpul*," Buber might say of a philosophical question that did not engage the individual. *Pilpul* was a word for the type of hair-splitting that became common when the study of the Talmud degenerated into sterile casuistry.

What impressed me most, though, was that, although not himself an observant Jew, Buber, at seventy-three years old, walked miles on a cold winter's night across Central Park rather than ride on the Sabbath in violation of the rules of the Seminary that sponsored his trip.

While in America, Buber contacted numerous old friends, including Albert Einstein, who spent many years at Princeton University before his death in 1955. Einstein and Buber were delighted to discover that they both liked Ellery Queen mystery stories! Later, Buber confided to me that Einstein was very depressed over the atomic bomb as a result of which Einstein refused an operation that might have saved his life. After the scientist's death, Buber wrote to Rudolf Kayser that he thought of Einstein often and despite the infrequency with which they communicated, when Einstein died he felt a great loss. Kayser replied that after meeting Buber at Princeton, Einstein had spoken of a fondness and admiration for him.

Buber was also a friend of the physicist Niels Bohr, who said to Buber in a conversation that the complementary theory of physics, whereby the basic elements could sometimes be seen as particles and sometimes as waves, was valid across the board so that even the verbs "to be" and "to know" have lost their simple, unambiguous meaning. When Bohr was named to the Order of the Elephant in Denmark and had to devise a family shield, he chose the motto *contraria sunt complementa*, a phrase close to Nicholas of Cusa's *coincidentia oppositorum*, which had informed Buber's thought from his doctoral dissertation on. Buber had an affinity for the oppositions of Heraclitus and for the Taoist yin and yang (he wrote a book on Taoism in 1924, the year after the publication of *Ich und Du*).

In fact, Buber had an abiding and lifelong interest in world religions. In the lecture on "Religion and Philosophy" that he gave before a large audience at Columbia University in the fall of 1951, Buber claimed that the personal manifestation of the divine is not decisive for the genuineness of religion, as in Epicurus, whose belief in a personal God did not bring him into full relationship with that God. Rather, what mattered was standing in relation to the divine with one's whole being, as the Buddha did:

> Even when the "Unoriginated" is not addressed with voice or soul, religion is still founded on the duality of I and Thou. Even when the philosophical act culminates in a vision of unity, philosophy is founded on the duality of subject and object.[6] The highest certainty in every religion is that the meaning of existence is open and accessible in the lived concrete, not above the struggle with reality, but in it.

At a luncheon at the Cathedral of Saint John the Divine in New York City, I asked Buber how he could make this statement about all religion in the face of the Hindu Vedanta, which, in its non-dualistic tradition, rejects the duality of I and Thou in favor of the One without Second, the identity of Brahman and Atman. "That is its philosophy," Buber replied. "Its religious reality is still the lived concrete." Buber rejected Reinhold Niebuhr's distinction between Western religion as historical and Eastern religion as nonhistorical. While in New York City, Buber met, through me, the great Zen scholar D. T. Suzuki, whom I had brought to Sarah Lawrence to speak. Buber and Suzuki had some wonderful conversations that I felt quite privileged to attend.

The religious, for Buber, must struggle to protect the lived concrete as the meeting place of the human and the divine against all those forms—metaphysics, gnosis, magic, politics—that threaten its quality of presentness and uniqueness. It must also reject historicizing the moment as merely past or technicizing it into a means to a future end. Meaning must not be won through any type of analytical, synthetic, or phenomenological investigation of and reflection upon the lived concrete, such as modern existentialist philosophies are given to, but only in the unreduced immediacy of the moment:

> Of course, he who aims at the experiencing of experience will necessarily miss the meaning, for he destroys the spontaneity of the mystery. Only he reaches the meaning who stands firm, without holding back or reservation, before the whole might of reality, and answers it in a living way.[7]

In contrast to Alfred North Whitehead, meanwhile, who, in *Religion in the Making* contrasted the "fear of God" of the Old Testament with the "love of God" of the New, Buber stressed that only the *beginning* of wisdom is the fear of God. The person who tries to begin with the love of God "does not love the real God who is, to begin with, dreadful and incomprehensible" but loves an idol that is easily shattered by reality. The person of faith does not settle down in the dread of God, as some modern theologians suggest, but he goes through it and only then is he directed to the concrete contextual situations of existence. He does not accept the concrete situation as "God-given" in its pure factuality. Rather, he may oppose it with all his force, but he will not remove himself from this situation as it actually is. To such a person "even the sublimest spirituality is an illusion if it is not bound to the situation."[8]

A key to Buber's understanding of all religions, implied in his response to my question about Vedanta, was his distinction between the philosophical bases of religions and their practical, concrete, relational realties. I-Thou, for Buber, finds its highest intensity and transfiguration in religious reality in which unlimited Being becomes, as a person, my partner. I-It finds its highest concentration and illumination in philosophical knowledge in which the subject is extracted from the lived togetherness of I and It and the It is detached into contemplated existing beings or contemplated Being itself.

Buber sought "the religious reality of the meeting with the Meeter, who shines through all forms and is himself formless, knows no image." Religious images, symbols, and concepts obstruct the road to God by appearing to be reality in themselves. Then comes round the hour of the philosopher, as I wrote in *The Life of Dialogue*, the *atheoi* like Socrates, who destroys the untrue images with his prayer and by so doing arouses the religious person and impels him to set forth across the God-deprived reality to a new meeting with the nameless Meeter.

Buber's sense of the religious life as encumbered by abstraction led him to sympathize with Camus, whom I called an atheist during a baccalaureate address that I gave when the University of Vermont awarded me an honorary doctorate. When I sent Buber a copy of this address, Buber replied, "Do not call Camus an atheist. He is one of the men who destroy the images of God that are no longer true. You know how I feel about them." Buber once referred to Camus, in a conversation with me, as "my friend." In 1952, Buber wrote to Camus that Camus's book *The Rebel* (*L'Homme revolte*) appeared to him "of such importance for human life in this hour" that he would like to recommend it to Mossad Bialik, the national publishing house of Israel, for publication in Hebrew translation.[9] Camus was gladdened and honored. He wrote Buber from Paris that he had read *I and Thou* with great admiration and profit and that he had not hoped for or expected Buber to agree with his writings. When Camus's book of essays *Resistance, Rebellion, and Death* was published in America, I. F. Stone, the editor of the journal *Dissent*, wrote an article on it titled "Albert Camus: The Life of Dialogue," which concluded with the statement, "Camus lived the only life worth living—the life of dialogue."[10]

Martin Buber came to the apartment where Eugenia and I were living in New York City on December 29, 1951, for my thirtieth birthday. Eugenia had baked a splendid devil's food cake for our evening together but, having eaten his main meal at lunchtime, Buber would not touch it. Nonetheless, he made much of my birthday, as he did of his own birthday a decade later at a very small family party at his home in Talbiyeh in Jerusalem that Eugenia and I attended. Ready to grant any wish I had during my birthday evening in New York City, Buber fell to talking about the sense he had that Plato and Jesus became present to him when he read their words. He cautioned me not to communicate what he was sharing in such a way that people would think that he meant something occult by it.

In the course of the evening I called my mother in Tulsa and put Buber on the phone. "You see, something came of our meeting in Jerusalem," Buber said to my mother. Something came of it indeed!

Buber was invited to teach at the University of Judaism, the West Coast branch of the Jewish Theological Seminary, a two-month position in Los Angeles that Buber accepted. Before Martin and his wife Paula left for the West Coast, I desperately wanted to finish some of the later chapters of *Martin Buber: The Life of Dialogue* to give Buber a chance to read them. I had developed the habit of typing voluminous notes from my reading on large 6" x 8" note cards with the result that I practically stymied my own efforts to get on with my book. Finally, in desperation, I opened a large drawer in my desk, stuffed all my note cards in it, and wrote five or six chapters of my book without consulting my notes at all! When I brought these chapters to Buber, he asked me, "Do you always write like this—in a sort of rapture?" He also told me he was interested in what I might be doing in five years. He suggested that I might be writing on ethics, which seems surprising in retrospect since Buber, if I recall correctly, did not think ethics a real subject at all!

At Rockefeller Hall at the University of Chicago, on his way west, Buber gave the Heidegger and Sartre portion of his lecture titled "Religion and Modern Thinking" that I had translated and that later, like the other lectures, was published in *Eclipse of God*. Arnold Bergstrasser, who had chaired my doctoral committee for the Committee on the History of Culture at the University of Chicago, wrote me about this lecture in particular: "America," he believed, though he may have been referring only to the Midwest, "is not yet aware of the questions that Buber was answering." After he had finished lecturing at Rockefeller Hall, Buber saw a woman that he knew from Frankfurt. Buber, true to form, left the small group of notables he was walking with, went up to her in the crowd, greeted her warmly, and talked with her for a long time in German.

Martin and Paula particularly wanted to see the Grand Canyon while in America, which made a great impression on them both. Los Angeles made less of an impression on Martin. "Los Angeles is indeed 'as unusual' as New York," he wrote to me on

January 24, 1952, "but not by far as important. Since yesterday we are living on the roof of this hotel and in a night such as this we are looking down on all the singularity of the town—utterly unable to see it as a person; it is an agglomeration of agglomerations. But of course seeing these mountains and this ocean together was a thing by itself."

The city of agglomerations, however, did not stop Buber from encountering those he met as individuals. Once in Los Angeles, when Buber was traveling some distance in a taxi, the taxi driver suddenly turned to him and said, "Mister, I've got something to ask you. The other day, I read that you don't have to get angry right away. What do you think about that?" Buber asked him where he had read it. "In a magazine," the taxi driver replied. "Don't laugh, but the guy who said it is seven hundred years old." "You mean, he lived seven hundred years ago?" Buber asked. "Yeah, that's what I said. Name of Francis . . . Francis? . . . Oh yes Francis of Assisi." "Oh, then you have read something good," said Buber, and told him about Saint Francis of Assisi. After paying and departing, Buber missed his eyeglass case and decided that the handsome case must have fallen out of his pocket in the cab. Twenty minutes later, as he was coming out of the building, he encountered the cab driver walking toward him, with the case in his hand. As Buber himself pointed out in telling the story, for such a driver time is money and gasoline is more money. Recognizing that, Buber said to him, "Thank you. That was good of you. You are a nice man." At this, the giant of a man put his arms around the diminutive Buber and declared, "Nobody has ever said that to me before."

Now that Buber was across the country, our correspondence continued much as it had while he was in Israel before we met in person. For Buber, as he wrote to me in January 1952, the "ultimate purpose of his philosophy" was to "save the relationship between man and his Thou from decay." This involved understanding how God relates to man. "As to your question about farness and nearness," he wrote in response to one of my letters, "I think that God's 'farness' (Cf. Psalm 10, 1) means that to those who do not want to be near to Him He replies by not giving to them anymore the experience of nearness. This, I think, is meant in Jeremiah 34:31 'God has given me to be seen from afar.' One who does turn toward God in dialogue perceives God as also 'turning' to him from His 'farness.'" Buber's novel *For the Sake of Heaven* addressed these themes in terms of faithfulness and freedom. Buber wrote to me at one point while in Los Angeles that he regarded *For the Sake of Heaven* as the most important of his Hasidic writings.

When Buber did not like something that I wrote, he was quick to tell me. I was, throughout our correspondence in this period, concerned with the problem of evil and the ways in which genuine dialogue might offer redemption. "If God, man, and the world are identical, there is no evil," I held. "If God is entirely transcendent to the world, evil is radical and unredeemable. If God is immanent and transcendent, evil is real and redeemable." Although he had written me that the redemption of evil was the very best theme I could have chosen for my dissertation, he rightly corrected my attempt to bring the problem of evil alone into valuation. "First of all," he wrote in late January 1952, "I cannot agree that the problem of evil is the central core of the problem of 'valuation.'" Of greater importance, Buber believed, was my claim that "the ultimate religious reality is a supravaluational acceptation." Turning toward God in dialogue, he told me, was turning not in the direction of the good since God is not the philosophical "good" but the "overgood." God, he wrote, is "superior to all duality or polarity."

In February 1952, I received two letters from the Jewish Peace Fellowship concerning the possibility of Buber's speaking to them when he returned to New York. They were very anxious to hear him speak, and I urged him to keep this engagement in mind. The Jewish Peace Fellowship was a serious group of pacifists with a real dedication to and genuine interest in discovering the relationship between Judaism and pacifism. Buber replied in March from Los Angeles with some reservation: "I am no pacifist," he wrote, "for I do not know at all whether in a given situation in which fighting had become necessary, I would not fight." As Buber once said to me, "One must choose between an 'ism,' including pacifism, and the concrete situation." On a personal note, he added that unlike me he could not have been a conscientious objector in the face of Hitler. "Of course, I am for peace with my whole heart, but not for the usual peace which only continues and prepares for war in a veiled form." Buber said, however, that he had nothing at all against discussing this with a small group in unreserved openness and proposed the evening of April 12. We met, accordingly, with a few members and leaders of the Jewish Peace Fellowship. One member asked Buber why Israel did not unilaterally disarm. "Because the first day the Bedouins would look on in amazement," Buber responded, "and the second day they would ride in."

Buber continued his guidance of my book while in Los Angeles, advising me to work on it a minimum of two hours a day without interruption "even if it should bore you sometimes" because "such a work demands from the spirit a particular kind of intensity and continuity." At the same time, we were continuing to prepare a manuscript of *The Eclipse of God* for Harper & Bros., which had requested several essays added to the manuscript in progress. Reflecting his concern that the book speak to a secular and Christian audience, he suggested that we not include those works, such as his essay *Imitation of God* (*Imitatio Dei*), which he thought unsuitable because they were "specifically Jewish," and *Eclipse* "should be meant for every man who is seriously interested in the subject." Buber was also much concerned about the problem of a concluding chapter, which later became "God and the Spirit of Man." "I have felt many times the need for it," he confessed, "but have not been able to write what I want to be said. I shall try again and hope to succeed, but I cannot yet tell when." "To you personally," he added, "(and what I am saying to you is, of course, for Eugenia too), I may explain that this chapter is, as it was, inclined to take the shape of a prayer, and I do not want to end this 'philosophical' book by a prayer."

Martin and Paula returned to New York from Los Angeles to spend some months in New York before returning to Israel. In his lecture at the City College of New York, Buber gave talks on the thought of Jung, Heidegger, and Sartre from his paper on "Religion and Modern Thinking." Jung, Buber held, was guilty of confining God within the immanence of human thought and of his own psychology, while Heidegger still had faint echoes of the transcendence of God in his concept of the future dawn of the holy. Because of this, Buber remarked to me just before he ascended the stage at one talk, "To me, Jung is more dangerous than Heidegger." This remark intrigued me since Heidegger was for a time an active member of the Nazi Party, which Buber detested and fought with all his being, while Jung was not.

Buber's travel and lecture schedule was beginning to wear on him. One night when I asked him questions about the "evil" urge—the *yetzer ha-ra* of the Talmud—and Hasidism, he said to me, lying down on the couch, "You don't understand, I really am tired!" Paula Buber, who had been traveling with Buber this entire trip, impressed me as an amazingly strong person. Joachim Wach had described Martin and Paula, after he had seen them at a European conference on the history of religion, as being like Blake's etchings of Job and his wife, and this proved to be the case. When I attempted to speak to Paula in German (she knew no English), she suggested that we wait until I had learned German better or she had learned English. In 1958 we did converse in

German during Buber's third visit to America, my German having improved through my work translating Buber's books into English.

Before Paula and Martin went back to Israel, the seminary had a large celebration in his honor. As his farewell lecture, Buber read "Hope for This Hour" in which he pointed to genuine dialogue between the nations as the embodiment of this hope. Reinhold Niebuhr was too ill to give the introductory lecture to a talk Buber gave at Carnegie Hall that he had been planning, but Paul Tillich came. Along with his own personal indebtedness to Buber, at Carnegie Hall Tillich expressed the view that he was undoubtedly more Greek than Buber. Some time later, at Brandeis University, an intense dialogue between Buber and Tillich took place that led Tillich, mistakenly, to conclude that Buber was angry with him, as he told me when I later asked him to contribute to the Buber section of *Philosophical Interrogations* that I was putting together. Buber's Carnegie Hall address was later included in a collection of important lectures of the year. Buber wanted to see it published in America, but not in a predominantly Jewish journal such as *Commentary*. In search of a suitable journal to publish "Hope for This Hour," I sent it to William Phillips, coeditor of *Partisan Review*, who at that time was my colleague at Sarah Lawrence College. Phillips's opinion, which I found surprising and never quite understood, was that Buber did not understand the reality of the Cold War. This response led Buber to write the little essay "Abstract and Concrete" that he included in his 1957 collected essays *Pointing the Way*.

On the morning that the Bubers were to take their plane back to Israel, we discovered that the apartment in Riverdale that we were renting for a year from Albert Lauterbach, who taught economics at Sarah Lawrence, had been robbed. The thief took many things of value that we owned. Eugenia and I were devastated. When I talked with Buber on the phone to say goodbye, I mentioned to him what had happened. "I could tell it from your voice," he said.

By the end of his trip, Buber's impression of Americans was rather muted. He remarked to me that people in America were "very polite," by which he did not mean to suggest that they engage in genuine dialogue.

At the end of April 1952, after his departure, I wrote a long letter to Buber expressing my gratitude. Though I didn't say so directly, I clearly missed him. "It is hard to believe that you are really gone," I wrote, "that I can no longer enter the Hotel Marcy and find you there at the door of Room 701 where you will invite me in and speak with me. I shall always be deeply grateful that my personal 'direction' so coincided with yours that I was in New York during the year of your visit. Eugenia and I were often unhappy when we saw how hard you had to work and how tired you became. But you have given a great deal to many, many persons while you were here, not merely lectures but wholly personally. You have given of yourself unbelievably, and that will certainly bear fruit in the life and thought of the persons with whom you came in contact, as with Eugenia and me. I only have a bad conscience that I have so often made demands on you when you were tired and that in the anxious knowledge of how short a time you would be here I lost the feeling for the present."

In this same letter, I wrote Buber about his book *Images of Good and Evil*, which he had sent me in manuscript in his own handwriting in the original German and which I had now read again in the English translation. I had eagerly awaited this book because it dealt with the very subject on which I had written my doctoral dissertation. "That is your penalty for writing on a living man!" Joachim Wach said to me. Eugenia found it Buber's most important book since *I and Thou*, and I was deeply impressed by its depth and simplicity and by the way in which it united the wisdom of the myths and the wisdom of personal experience:

"I shall never cease to be astonished at how each of your works expresses something really new and yet remains within the unity of your thought," I told him. "But this work says something new that I could not even have foreseen when I treated your earlier works from the standpoint of this problem."

After Buber's visit Eugenia tried to communicate to Barbara O'Donnel, her best friend, who lived in Ohio, something of what meeting Buber had meant to her:

> Martin Buber is greater than his books. And this, it seems to me, is a very telling statement in itself because his books are very great. Martin Buber is greater than his books because he lives what he has written and the living embodiment of the word is a more marvelous achievement than the writing down of the word.
>
> I have seen him in many different situations and always I have received the same impression of him—a real human being interested in just this life we all live and in how to hallow just this very life. I have never understood what it means to be a real human being, but Martin Buber has now shown me. He is, secondly, a religious man, not a spiritual man or a mystic. The difference is very important. . . . Finally, I would say about Martin Buber that he is a man to whom one could tell anything about one's life and feel positive that he would not be shocked and he would not judge.
>
> He is a short man, built stockily. He has a remarkably fine head, very imposing with his white beard that makes him look like a prophet. His brown eyes are the most outstanding physical feature that he has. I shall never forget the look he gave me when I first met him. I would not call his eyes penetrating, but rather open. Sometimes when he looks at you, you feel that you are looking right into the man and you feel a sudden great, comforting warmth. He confirms the other person. He smiles and laughs often; often when he smiles, his face has a charming

disarmed look. I have several times seen him with a stern look that passed quickly, and he is always serious. This last doesn't bother me at all; in fact, it is a relief to me.

I know that Martin Buber has suffered very much, but his suffering has knit him together into a whole human being. Often a suffering human being is like a sick or crippled human being. But not so with him. He turns to and responds to human encounter with his whole being in an absolute, consistent steadiness. I heard him say that the teacher's function is "to give the student trust, just to be there for him, like a mother is for the child." That is what Martin Buber does. He gives one trust.

5

Sartre, Heidegger, Jung, and Scholem

In *Images of Good and Evil*, Buber used both biblical and Zoro-astrian myths, which embody directly without passing through any conceptual form what has taken place in the countless human encounters with evil. Buber coupled the primordial mythical intu-ition of Zoroastrianism with directly experienced reality in such a way as to extend and deepen his philosophical anthropology. Just as importantly, Buber designated two stages of evil, which he had never done before: a first in which evil grows directly out of "decisionlessness," the failure to find the direction to God by responding with one's whole being to the concrete situation; and a second in which evil takes the form of a decision made but not with the whole being.

In the first stage, unable to bear the difficult path of bringing itself toward unity, the soul clutches at any object past which the vortex happens to carry it and casts its passion upon it, grasping, devouring, compelling, seducing, exploiting, humiliating, tor-turing, and destroying. This vision of man bowled over as much by possibility as by infinitude is very similar to Kierkegaard's concept of the origin of sin and the fall in *The Concept of Dread*. It also stands in a direct line with that threat of infinity that brought the fourteen-year-old Buber close to suicide: the tempta-tion of the creative man to lose himself in infinity, about which

Buber wrote when he was twenty-five in "The Day of Looking Back." In this essay, written at fifty, Buber recalled how Paula had set a limit to his own delusion and madness and helped him make a real decision as a young man with what he called in *I and Thou* the "fiery stuff" of one's possibilities that circles around the person who must give direction to the "evil urge" of self-annihilation.

In the second stage of evil, the repeated experiences of indecision merge into a fixation that produces a crisis of confirmation. In this stage, that Yes with which others speak to a person, and with which he can speak to himself to free him from the anxiety of loneliness, which is a foretaste of death, is no longer spoken. In a pinch, one can do without the confirmation of others, but not without the confirmation of oneself. Those who become pathologically fragile in their relationship to themselves extinguish the image of what they are intended to be in favor of an absolute self-affirmation that says, "What I say is true because I say it and what I do is good because I do it." It was undoubtedly Buber's experience with the Nazis and with the war in Palestine that led him to deepen his view of evil to include this second stage.

The great significance of this second stage of evil for Buber's thought is its concrete base in human existence that makes understandable such extreme phenomena as Hitler and the Nazis without resorting to the dogma of original sin or agreeing with Sartre's assertion that the events of the early twentieth century made it necessary to recognize evil as absolute and unredeemable. Less than ten years later, during the trial of Adolf Eichmann, looking at the pictures and reading the description of Eichmann during his trial, I thought of what Buber had asserted in *Good and Evil* about the product of this crystallized inner division: "They are recognizable, those who dominate their own self-knowledge, by the spastic pressure of the lips, the spastic tension of the muscles of the hand and the spastic tread of the foot."[1]

In his lecture on Sartre and Heidegger, which he delivered in New York, Buber quoted Sartre as saying that there is no universe other than that of human subjectivity and that man must recognize himself as the being through whom the universe exists. This sounded like the thesis of a resurrected idealism, Buber argued. If God is silent toward man and man toward God, "then something has taken place not in human subjectivity, Sartre to the contrary, but in Being itself. It would be worthier not to explain it to oneself with sensational and incompetent sayings, such as that of the death of God, but to endure it as it is and at the same time to move existentially toward a new happening, toward that event in which the word between heaven and earth will again be heard."[2] Sartre's conclusion that it was now up to us to give life meaning and value "is almost exactly what Nietzsche said, and it has not become any truer since then," Buber held.

One can believe in and accept a meaning or value; one can set it as a guiding light over one's life if one has discovered it, not if one has invented it. It can be for me an illuminating meaning, a direction-giving value, only if it has been revealed to me in my meeting with Being, not if I have freely chosen it for myself among the existing possibilities and perhaps have in addition decided with some fellow creatures: This shall be valid from now on.

In the original German manuscript of "Religion and Modern Thinking" there is a footnote in which Buber linked Sartre's statement, "If God is dead, all things are allowable," with the peripheral Islamic political-religious sect of the Assassins (from whom we also get the words assassin and hashish, since they were "enjoyers of hashish"), the group that lived in the mountains and murdered passersby and whose secret was that they did not believe in God. Nietzsche took over their teaching from the noted Orientalist Joseph von Hammer-Purgstall and Sartre from Nietzsche. Since the Assassins were clearly a type of antinomian Gnostic sect, I found this connection between them and these modern philosophers particularly fascinating. Nonetheless, I objected to Buber in a letter that he could not connect Sartre with them, since Sartre explicitly quotes Dostoevsky as a source for his existentialism in "Existentialism Is a Humanism." But where Dostoevsky drew back from the consequences, Sartre accepted them without blinking an eye. Dostoevsky himself attributed a similar Gnostic antinomianism to Ivan Karamazov, who held that if there were no God, values were not merely baseless, but one was morally bound to do the opposite of what had formerly been the moral law. Buber had written to me from Los Angeles agreeing that Sartre probably did not know Hammer-Purgstall's book *The Assassins* (1818) in which it is written "That nothing is true and everything permissible remained the ground of their secret teaching." Sartre "might have heard the Assassins from another source," he suggested. In response to my objection, however, Buber had me eliminate this footnote on the Assassins from the English version of his essay.

In contrast to Sartre, Heidegger did not even hold that existentialism is humanism. He saw man as the shepherd of Being who cannot create the house of Being through his thought, but that thought can lead the humanness of man in history into the realm where what is whole and holy (*das Heile*) arises. This can only take place, however, when "being has illuminated itself and has then been experienced truthfully." Buber pointed out that in Heidegger's view it is precisely in *human* thought about truth that Being becomes illuminated. This, according to Buber, was incompatible with the real transcendence of the divine. Being or Beings have always stepped into relation with us of their own will and allowed us to enter into relation with them. "Being turned toward us, descended to us, showed itself to us, spoke to us in the immanence. . . . That has always distinguished religion from magic."[3] God wills to need man as an independent partner in dialogue, as a comrade in work. "God does not let Himself be conjured, but he also will not compel." Through man's giving or denying himself, "the whole man with the decision of his whole being" may have an immeasurable part in the actual revelation or hiddenness of the divine.

But there is no place between heaven and earth for an influence of concept-clarifying thought. He whose appearance can be affected or co-affected through such a modern magical influence clearly has only the name in common with Him whom we men, basically in agreement despite all the differences in our religious teachings, address as God.

Sartre brought Nietzsche's expression of the death of God to a reductio ad absurdum, Buber contended, through his postulate of the free invention of meaning and value, whereas Heidegger has created out of it a concept of a rebirth of God out of the thought of truth which falls into the enticing net of historical time.

Buber also offered a compelling critique of Carl Jung, one that generated a fruitful debate between them. In May 1952, Buber wrote me from Zurich and told me that he had completed the German original of "God and the Spirit of Man," his concluding essay in *The Eclipse of God*, on the long boat trip that he had taken to recover from the overexertions of his half-year in America. Buber finished the final page of "God and the Spirit of Man" the last day on the boat. "Physically, I did not feel well," Buber added, "nor did my wife—the air-conditioned cabin, devoid of windows, was terribly lacking in air and light, but the spirit was with me faithfully."

In "God and the Spirit of Man," Buber pointed to two stages of philosophizing, the first of which he found beneath much modern philosophy, particularly, as a debate between them developed, in that of Carl Jung. In this stage, the human spirit fuses its conception of the Absolute with itself "until, finally, all that is over against, everything that accosts us and takes possession of us, all partnership of existence, is dissolved in free-floating subjectivity,"[4] and one in which the human spirit annihilates conceptually the absoluteness of the Absolute and in so doing destroys its own absoluteness. Now the spirit can no longer exist as an independent essence but only as a product of human individuals which they contain and secrete. Buber also pointed to two pseudoreligious counterparts of the reality of the relation of faith—controlling and unveiling, magic and gnosis. In magic, one celebrates rites without being turned to the Thou and without really meeting its presence. Magic wishes to control the power it conjures up, rather than relating to the complexity of concrete events. In gnosis, which Buber saw as underlying the kabbalistic Hasidism of Gershom Scholem, the power of the intellect is used to unveil and display the "divine mysteries," the holy *It*.

Genuine prayer, in contrast, asks that the divine Presence become dialogically perceivable. The simplest presupposition for such prayer—"the readiness of the whole man for this Presence, simple turned-towardness, unreserved spontaneity"—is destroyed today by overconsciousness that I am *praying*, that *I* am praying. He who is not present perceives no Presence, and modern man cannot be spontaneously present so long as he holds back a part of his *I* that does not enter into the action of prayer with the rest of his person, an *I* to which the prayer is an object. This was "the subjective knowledge of the one turning-towards *about* his turning-towards."[5]

What is in question with both modern philosophy and modern religion is not the choice between I-Thou and I-It, for Buber, but whether the I-Thou remains the architect, the I-It the helper. If the I-Thou does not command, then it is already disappearing. Yet precisely this disappearance of "I-Thou," Buber held, was the character of the hour:

In our age the I-It relation, gigantically swollen, has usurped, practically uncontested, the mastery and the rule. The I of this relation, an I that possesses all, makes all, succeeds with all, this

I that is unable to say Thou, unable to meet being essentially, is the lord of the hour. This selfhood that has become omnipotent, with all the It that surrounds it, can naturally acknowledge neither God nor any genuine Absolute which manifests itself to man as of non-human origin. It steps in between and shuts us off from the light of heaven.[6]

In his essay "Martin Buber and the Philosophies of Existence" in *The Philosophy of Martin Buber*, the distinguished French philosopher Jean Wahl misunderstood Buber's metaphor of the "eclipse of God" as introducing an "almost gnostic" conception of a strange and hindering element. What Buber was saying was not that God is *hidden*—the *Deus absconditus* of the Gnostics—but that God is *hiding*. "The eclipse of the light of God is no extinction," Buber concluded in "God and the Spirit of Man"; "even tomorrow that which has stepped in between may give way." If the I-Thou relationship has gone into the catacombs today, no one can infer how much greater power it will re-emerge with tomorrow. As Buber had said of the work of the suffering servant hidden in the depths of history, here he asserted that the most important events of history are the beginnings of new epochs, determined by forces previously invisible or disregarded. "Each age is, of course, a continuation of the preceding one, but a continuation can be confirmation or it can be refutation."

Buber, meanwhile, had been wrestling with the problem of subjectivism and its outcome in I-It relations for some time. In 1934, Buber took part in the Jungian Eranos Conference in Ascona, Switzerland, and he would have done so again in 1935 had it not been for the Nazi restrictions on his lecturing. Buber had, for many years, close friendships with many Jungian analysts, the chief of which was with Hans Trüb, but in 1951 Buber devoted the second half of his sharply critical essay "Religion and Modern Thinking" to Jung. Buber, as we have seen, held Jung to be more dangerous than Heidegger. For him, Jung's gnostic transformation seemed to contribute far more in actuality to the human responsibility for the "eclipse of God than Heidegger's 'thought-magic.'" When this controversy between Buber and Jung came to public attention in 1951, many people in Europe, America, and Israel were shocked. The traditional enemy of religion was assumed to be Freud while Jung was hailed as its great friend. Many of Jung's followers were very close to Buber and vice versa, and not a few considered themselves disciples of both men who, they believed, shared a common concern with "modern man in search of a soul." What is more, Jung's "collective unconscious," or "objective psyche," has an unmistakable transpersonal, objective, numinous, and awe-inspiring nature that led Jung to identify it with Rudolf Otto's *Mysterium Tremendum*. In "Religion and Modern Thinking," Buber himself called Jung "the leading psychologist of our day" and pointed out that Jung had made religion, in its historical and biographical forms, the subject of comprehensive observations.

What Buber criticized Jung for is that, for all his disclaimers, "he oversteps with sovereign license the boundaries of psychology" by defining religion as "a living relation to psychical events which . . . take place . . . in the darkness of the psychical hinterland."[7] Buber objected that Jung conceives of God in general as an "autonomous psychic content." That these are not merely psychological statements, as Jung would claim, but metaphysical ones, Buber showed by quoting Jung's statements that otherwise "God is indeed not real; for then He nowhere impinges upon our lives" and that God is "for our psychology . . . a function of the unconscious" as opposed to the "orthodox conception" according to which "God exists for Himself."[8] Psychologically, for Jung, this meant "that one is unaware that the action arises from one's own inner self." Psychology becomes to Jung the only admissible metaphysic while also remaining an empirical science. "But," Buber objected, "it cannot be both at once."

Buber also criticized Jung's understanding of the soul through which alone the collective unconscious, the sphere of the archetypes, can enter into our experience. "The real soul has without question producing powers in which the primal energies of the human race have individually concentrated," commented Buber, who was certainly no stranger to these matters in his early concern with myth and with Jewish peoplehood. "But it can never legitimately make an assertion out of its own creative powers but only out of a binding real relationship to a truth which it articulates." Modern consciousness, with which Jung clearly identified himself, "abhors faith and . . . the religions that are founded on it," and turns instead with its "most intimate and intense experience" to the soul as the only sphere that can be expected by man to harbor the divine. The new psychology thus "proclaims the new religion, the only one which can still be true, the religion of pure psychic immanence." What is more, it turns to the soul, in Jung's own words "in the Gnostic sense," as the new court that replaces conscience by the unity of good and evil. This union of opposites, Buber pointed out, is the mature expression of a tendency characteristic of Jung from the beginning of his intellectual life. "In a very early writing, which was printed but was not sold to the public, it appears in direct religious language as the profession of an eminent *Gnostic* god (Abraxas), in whom good and evil are bound together and, so to speak, balance each other." In modern mandala dreams "the place of the deity," Jung explains, "appears to be taken by the wholeness of man," which Jung calls the "Self."[9]

Although Jung avoided the deification of man in some places, in others the Self, the marriage of good and evil, is elevated to the highest possible place as the new "Incarnation" whose prospective appearance Jung repeatedly intimates. "If we should like to know," says Jung, "what happens in the case in which the idea of God is no longer projected as an autonomous essence, then this is the answer of the unconscious soul: the unconscious creates the idea of a deified or divine man." "This figure," commented Buber, "is the final form of the Gnostic god, descended to earth as the realization of 'the identity of God and man,' which Jung once professed."[10]

What concerned Buber about Jung was not his creed or belief or metaphysics but what happened to the relation of faith itself in actual human existence if one followed Jung's theology to its conclusions. "Whatever may be the case concerning God," Buber paraphrased Jung, "the important thing for the man of modern consciousness is to stand in no further relation of faith to God." When one is called to a work that one has not done or fulfilled, a task that one knows to be one's own, one knows what it means to say that one's conscience smites one: for conscience is the voice that compares what one is with what one is called to become. Jung dispenses with this court of conscience in favor of the soul integrated in the Self as the unification, in an all-encompassing wholeness, of good and evil. Jung sees the Self as including the world, to be sure, but "the others," declared Buber, "are included only as contents of the individual soul that shall, just as an individual soul, attain its perfection through individuation." All beings who are "included" in this way in myself are, in fact, only possessed as an It.[11]

Only then when, having become aware of the unincludable otherness of a being, I renounce all claim to incorporating it in any way within me or making it a part of my soul, does it truly become Thou for me. In genuine dialogue, one cannot reduce the dialogical other to the contents of one's own consciousness. Buber characterized the way that he advanced in opposition to Jung's as one "which leads from the soul which places reality in itself to the soul which enters reality."[12] The biblical scholar Benjamin Uffenheimer once said that Buber was ready to enter into dialogue with Jung but that Jung did not want a dialogue with Buber—a statement that is borne out by the tone of all of Jung's correspondence on the subject.

When I suggested to Buber that he publish Jung's reply to Buber's criticism in *Eclipse of God*, Buber said he had no right to do so. We did, however, give the reader the German and English references for finding Jung's reply—something Gershom Scholem never did for Buber in the many places he published his critique of Buber's interpretation of Hasidism.[13] The strangest thing about Jung's reply to Buber was that he ascribed Buber's criticism of him to Buber's Jewish "orthodoxy," a statement the irony of which no one could be unaware of who knew the criticism from Orthodox Jewish scholars that Buber had to live through for fifty years, particularly in Palestine. In response to Jung's argument, Buber remarked that as a rule he did not bring his own beliefs into the discussion but held them in check for the sake of human dialogue. "But it must be mentioned here for the sake of full clarity that my own belief in revelation," he wrote, "which is not mixed up with any orthodoxy, does not mean that I believe that finished statements about God were handed down from heaven to earth. Rather," he stated, "it means that the human substance is melted by the spiritual fire which visits it, and there now breaks forth from it a word, a statement, which is human in its meaning and form, human conception and human speech, and yet witnesses to Him who stimulated it and to His will. We are revealed to ourselves—and cannot express it other than as something revealed."[14]

Why Buber saw Jung's modern Gnosticism as more dangerous than Heidegger's thought-magic—for Heidegger represented the second of the two perspectives on religion Buber critiqued in "Religion and Modern Man"—is made unmistakably clear in the final paragraph of Buber's reply to Jung:

> The psychological doctrine which deals with mysteries without knowing the attitude of faith toward mystery is the modern manifestation of Gnosis. Gnosis is not to be understood as an historical category but as a universal one. It—and not atheism

which rejects the hitherto existing images of God—*is the real antagonist of the reality of faith*. Its modern manifestation concerns me particularly not only because of its massive pretensions, but also in particular because of its resumption of the Carpocratian motif. This motif, which it teaches as psychotherapy, is that of mystically deifying the instincts instead of hallowing them in faith [italics added].[15]

The issue Buber put before Jung, at its simplest, was this: Either truth is reduced to the psychic and becomes mere tautology or the psychic is elevated to Truth and becomes a false hypostasizing. For Jung is not a Gnostic—they traditionally believed in a totally transcendent God—but a *modern* Gnostic whose touchstone of reality is the collective psyche, the Self.

For all the numinous, guiding quality of Jung's collective unconscious it is still an *It* and not a *Thou*. It can neither be addressed as Thou nor can one live in dialogue contending with It, as could man with the transcendent yet present God of the Hebrew Bible. It certainly has a quality of overagainstness: it can never be identified with the conscious person or even with the personal unconscious. But there is no mutuality, no give and take, no sense that Jung's God needs man for the very purpose for which he created him. Indeed, Jung's God is not the Creator but a demiurge finding his place within a larger order as Zeus did within the Greek cosmos; for Jung's ultimate touchstone of reality is not the autonomous content of the unconscious psyche that he calls "Self" but the unconscious psyche itself. The placing of the divine in the unconscious, however archetypally and universally conceived, psychologizes God *and* reality, robbing our meeting with "the things of this world" of any revelatory power other than the mimetic reflection of our forgotten and buried inner truths. If Jung had not asserted the psyche as the *exclusive* touchstone of reality, he could have bestowed great honor upon a realm that undoubtedly has profound meaning, whether that of the shadow, the anima, the animus, the Great Mother, or any of the other life-symbols that slumber in our depths, without hypostasizing that realm into an inverted Platonic universal and elevating this larger-than-life-sized sphere to the now-empty throne of the Absolute.

In 1948, meanwhile, the great scholar of Jewish mysticism Gershom Scholem, who single-handedly made the study of the Kabbalah into a science, had come to the University of Chicago and visited my teacher Joachim Wach, whom he had known in Europe. When I met with Scholem alone to discuss my interests, he said, "There is nothing to learning Hebrew. You study it for 13 hours a day for five years and then you know it. Otherwise what can you do but quote Scholem, Scholem, Scholem!" At this point, Scholem got so excited that he took the leather eyeglass case that he was holding in his hand and placed it on his nose—an unforgettable image! Later, when I got to know Paula Buber personally, she told me that Martin and she invited Scholem to come to dinner when he was twenty-one. At that time, according to both Martin and Paula, Scholem was a sort of intellectual cowboy. When dinner was over and Scholem had left, Rafael and Eva— the two Buber children—exclaimed, "How could you invite such a man to dinner?" "Someday he will be a great scholar," Paula replied.

When I was invited to edit *The Philosophy of Martin Buber* volume of the Library of Living Philosophers, I was told that it would be a "labor of love." A "labor of love" is indeed what it was. Paul Arthur Schilpp, the editor of the series, was given half time off by Northwestern University for his work whereas I, who spent ten years editing the Buber volume, received nothing at all. Schilpp wanted the title page of the Buber volume to read, "Edited by Paul Arthur Schilpp, Assisted by Maurice Friedman," my "assistance" to be duly acknowledged by Schilpp in his preface ("a typical

German practice," Ernst Simon said to me). Since all Schilpp had done was send out the letters of invitation, I rejected this proposal and insisted that we both be listed as editors—for which Schilpp never forgave me!

One of the invitations that I sent out requesting an essay for the volume was to Scholem. He rejected the invitation but put us in touch with one of his students—Rivka Schatz-Uffenheimer, wife of the biblical scholar Benjamin Uffenheimer. Rivka wrote an essay on Buber's Hasidic chronicle-novel *For the Sake of Heaven* with a paragraph of great appreciation at the beginning and the end ("If you have not read it at least twice, you have not read it at all," she wrote) with forty pages of solid Scholemite criticism in between. I went to see Scholem in Jerusalem and asked him once again if he did not perhaps have something already written that he could contribute to the Buber volume. "I have," he replied, "but I would not give it to you."

"Why not?" I queried.

"Because it [the volume] allows the philosopher to have the last word," Scholem rejoined.

In this, Scholem was correct. Every volume of the Library of Living Philosophers, with the exception of the two that were published when the philosopher was no longer living (John Dewey being one), concluded with a section of "Replies to My Critics." Buber's replies, which I translated, devoted a whole section to his interpretation of Hasidism. Buber did not offer any replies to Scholem, but they had, for many years, been engaged in a debate about the "mystical" aspects of Hasidism. Scholem's first book in English, *Major Trends in Jewish Mysticism*, concludes with a chapter on Hasidism that is in all essential respects in accord with Buber's approach. Although Hasidism was based in the Lurianic Kabbalah, everything is psychologized, everything becomes a story. Never had so many genuine charismatics been grouped together as in the early generations of Hasidism, Scholem attested.

But Scholem was too much of an intellectual historian to leave it at that, and this is where his major difference from Buber emerged and developed. Buber held that the true life of the Hasidim was best captured by the tales of the Hasidim that he spent a large part of his life editing and retelling. Scholem discounted the tales in comparison to the formal teachings of Hasidism because the teachings were written down immediately whereas the tales were not written down till fifty years later. In his response to this criticism, Buber pointed out that when the tales were written down was not essential since this was at a time when there was fear lest they be lost for good. For Sufism, too, the tales were not written down till a later time. For Scholem, the intellectual historian, the written word was paramount. For Buber, the philosopher of dialogue, as for my friend Abraham Joshua Heschel, the scion of eight generations of zaddikim going back to the Maggid of Mezritch, the spoken word was more important than the written.

Scholem had a critique of Buber's Hasidism which Norman Podhoretz published in *Commentary*. This, in effect, gave Scholem the last word that he wanted, for Buber's reply, which I also translated, was not published by *Commentary* till a year and a half after Scholem's piece, by which time it had, of course, lost its effect as a reply. In his essay for *Commentary*, Scholem tells of how he said to Buber that he would bring to him the results of his researches when they were ready. When he did so, according to Scholem's account in the essay, Buber stated, emphasizing every word, "If that is the case, dear Scholem, I have wasted forty years on Hasidism, because it does not at all interest me." In quoting this, Scholem felt he had demonstrated how little Buber respected or cared for the scientific research that he had done.

What Scholem missed entirely was that Buber was saying that *his* Hasidism was not at all what Scholem had presented to him. Buber's response was printed in *The Knowledge of Man* (in my translation) as "The Word That Is Spoken." Buber began his essay, which originally appeared in the September 1963 issue of *Commentary*, with a long section on "the two different ways in which a great tradition of religious faith can be rescued from the rubble of time and brought back into the light": that of historical scholarship and that of faithfully and adequately communicating the vitality and power of this faith. The latter "approach derives from the desire to convey to our own time the force of a former life of faith and to help our age renew its ruptured bond with the Absolute." For this approach, it is necessary to have an adequate knowledge of the tradition in all its spiritual and historical connections. It is not necessary to present all of a tradition, but only a selection in which the vitalizing element was embodied, a selection based not on objective knowledge but "upon the reliability of the person making the selection in the face of criteria; for what appeared to be mere 'subjectivity' to the detached scholar can sooner or later prove to be necessary to the process of renewal." The scholar, Buber held, "should not be expected to turn away from the traditional reports concerning the life of the pious in order to give primary emphasis to the theoretical doctrine to which the founder and his disciples appealed for their authority." Even in the founding of the world's great religions what was essential was not a doctrine but an event that was at once life and word. When, as in Hasidism, religious life reaches back to a much earlier doctrine in order to establish its legitimacy, it is not the old teaching as such that engenders a new life of faith in a later age but rather the context of personal and communal existence in which a far-reaching transformation of the earlier teachings takes place.[16]

While Hasidism based itself on the Kabbalah, it took over from the Kabbalah only what it needed "for the theological foundation of an enthusiastic but not overexalted life in responsibility" for the piece of world entrusted to one. In the place of Kabbalah's esoterically regulated meditations, Hasidism endowed each action with strength of intention, not according to any prescriptions but in response to the moment. The "simple man" of the original *devotio*, who possesses neither rabbinic nor kabbalistic learning, is held in honor in Hasidism because he serves God with his whole being. "Where the mystic vortex circled, now stretches the way of man." In Hasidism, *devotio* has absorbed and overcome gnosis. "This must happen ever again," Buber concluded, "if the bridge over the chasm of being is not to fall in."

> I am against gnosis because and insofar as it alleges that it can report events and processes within the divinity. I am against it because and insofar as it makes God into an object in whose nature and history one knows one's way about; I am against it because in the place of the personal relation of the human person to God it sets a communion-rich wandering through an upper world, through a multiplicity of more or less divine spheres.[17]

For Buber, Gnosis attempts to include God in the structure of knowledge erected on the base of the I-It relation, a structure that "claims the absolute legitimacy of the transmutation in an allegedly final valid appeal of the 'known' *mysterium*." This ultimately signifies the annihilation of lived concreteness *and* of creation, thereby offending not only the transcendent but also human existence.

For thirty years, I conducted discussions of Buber's Hasidic tales at my home, the last ten years with my former wife Eugenia Friedman who knows the tales even better than I do. Together, we worked systematically through *The Early Masters* and *The Later Masters*, taking one Hasidic master at a time and asking who in the group (which at times was as many as fifty people but toward the end only five or six) wanted to read aloud a tale that had struck her or him, and then to say why he or she had picked this particular tale, which was usually for personal rather than academic reasons. When Eugenia and I felt that the group has discussed a tale as much as it wanted to, we asked that person to read the tale aloud again as a conclusion to the discussion.

Out of these tales and meetings grew one of my books—*A Dialogue with Hasidic Tales*—based on Buber's selections and our discussions. The subtitle of this book, which I had actually wanted to be the main title, was *Hallowing the Everyday*. The act of hallowing, for Buber "a deed of the everyday that prepares the messianic completion," was central to the I-Thou relations established in the Hasidic tales:

> The great *kavana* is not joined to any particular selection of the prescribed: everything that is done with *kavana* can be the right, the redeeming act. Each action can be the one on which all depends: what is decisive is only the strength, the concentration with which I do it.[18]

Hallowing all that one does means to exchange a casual for an essential relation to what one does.

In the conclusion that I wrote for the *Leo Baeck Annual* on the controversy between Scholem and Buber over the interpretation of Hasidism, I cited the well-known Talmudic dictum, "Every controversy that takes place for the sake of heaven will endure." The controversy between Scholem and Buber will endure, I asserted, without, as so many such controversies do, the need to pronounce either Scholem or Buber right or wrong.

6

The Life of Dialogue

Letters Following Buber's First Visit

Buber and I kept up what I felt was an exhilarating correspondence after his return to Jerusalem as I grappled to understand and thus better explain his work. I was, at the time, as I
still remain, fascinated by Buber's understanding of the dialogue
between God and man in the Talmud. "Would it not be correct to
say that the reciprocity of the I-Thou relationship implies some
action on the part of God," I asked him in a letter in 1952, "in
response to the action of man, as a father may become angry with
a son without ceasing to love him, or may realize that the son is
not open to relationship and may bide his time without pressur-
ing him until the son is open? I realize, of course, that one may not
deduce an action from God from a philosophical proposition."
Will Herberg, a scholar and personal friend, reported to me that
Buber had told him that Buber understood God's revelation not in
terms of God's presence at Mount Sinai but in terms of Abraham's
turning toward God on the way to Sinai. Herberg felt that this
statement was a key to Buber's whole attitude toward revelation,
and for him this implied that Buber did not identify himself with
"normative" Judaism, with Judaism of the tradition.

Herberg's characterization suggested to me a vision of Abraham as one whom God caused to stray from his home and to
wander in an unknown way toward an unknown goal to which

the God of the way led him. This seemed to accord, I told Buber, with his interpretation of the Talmudic phrase that God spoke, "*ehyeh asher ehyeh*" ("I shall be there as I shall be there"), and with Buber's thoughts on the dialogue between God and man in "The Biblical Dialogue between Heaven and Earth," where he had written, "Though his coming appearance resembles no earlier one, we shall recognize again our cruel and merciful God."[1] In a sense, I agreed with Herberg that Abraham's journey was a key to Buber's attitude toward revelation, but I did not agree that Buber deemphasized the Sinai Covenant, given his interpretations of that covenant in *Koenigtum Gottes, Moses,* and *The Prophetic Faith.* I was especially curious to know whether Buber would distinguish between his interpretations of the tradition and his personal attitudes. Buber replied succinctly distinguishing between the spirit of Judaism implicit in Abraham's turning toward God and the content of God's laws once Abraham had met God face to face: "What you say about the spirit of Judaism and Sinai I cannot accept in these terms. What has been given on Sinai is not a special form but rather a special content, meaning a 'constitution.'" For Buber, the spirit of Judaism was manifest in the eternal revelation of the dialogue between God and Man. The revelation of God through the laws, while central to the tradition's constitution, did not contain or circumscribe this greater revelation. "This means simply one's experience is given him really just now," Buber wrote. "Of course, this personal receiving leads one to the understanding of the great revelations, but the primary fact is not the latter. . . . Eternal revelation means the Presence."

In the case of Abraham, the important moment was his decision to turn toward God, to move in the direction of God on Sinai, and then to enter relation with God. As Buber put it to me, "direction is, relation happens, direction is unilateral (from man to God), relation, bilateral (mutual). I take up the direction, I partake in the relation. Direction is not meeting but going out to meet."

The individual "conscience," which I suggested to Buber calls one to God, "is human and can be mistaken, it is a thing of 'fear and trembling,' it can only try to hear. I would never define conscience as a divine spark," he added in response to the metaphor I had put to him:

> Terms of assurance should not be introduced here, nothing in human life is just exempt of tragedy. The purpose of my unique-ness may be felt more or less dimly, it cannot be sensed. The objective direction to it does not mean a sensible aim. It is not as if I first become aware and then take the direction—I become aware in taking the direction. More precisely: in responding to God, in taking the direction to Him I become aware, in some measure, of the person meant for me in Creation.

"Of course," he added, "there is not such a thing as a 'separate continuing awareness in me'" such as the spark of divine con-science, "and it cannot be." It was always important to Buber to reject such subjectivist concepts as "divine spark" within the self, as his critique of Jung implied, since "One's uniqueness is not a 'substantive entity inside one'—potentiality never is, and so not even a chosen potentiality." In the individual's relation to God, the invitation to dialogue was always key since "God *does not want to compel* the sinner to turn to Him."

I had not, as we wrote in mid-1952, yet come to understand Buber's attitude toward revelation as present awareness of the Presence clearly enough. I thought that Buber had added to his conception of revelation as expressed in *I and Thou* a further belief that one can receive revelation through making present the awareness of the Presence that was symbolically or mythically expressed at Sinai and the burning bush. I was beginning to see that one comes to understand the great revelation through one's own revelations, but that one's own revelations are really unique

THE LIFE OF DIALOGUE   81

revelations in the present rather than participation in biblical revelations of the past. A dialogical revelation with God could no
more reproduce the experience of Abraham than one could come
from a discrete inner spark.

In September 1952, I received a response from William Phillips, the editor of *Partisan Review,* to Buber's essay "Hope for This
Hour," which critiqued both subjectivism and existentialism in
modern philosophy. Phillips's response, which was that Buber
did not sufficiently understand the realities of the Cold War, did
not suggest either understanding or careful reading of Buber's
essay. It was my belief that since Phillips had taught a good deal
of Sartre in his courses, he may perhaps have identified "existentialism" exclusively with Sartre and was not prepared to embrace
Buber's dialogical vision of existentialism. As part of his critique
of existentialist philosophy, Buber defined "reflexion" (*Rückbie-
gung*) as "bending back on oneself," as not having the other in
mind in his or her otherness and particularity. Phillips's response
to Buber inspired Buber to write a very short philosophical and
political treatment of the subject of his dialogical anthropology
in "Pointing the Way." In a letter in which Buber agreed that "a
man who as you say teaches a good deal of Sartre obviously likes
him and then he must either dislike me or (preferably) ignore
me," he also wrote that "there are three degrees of reflection": (1)
the indispensable reflecting on my inner (introspective) experience; (2) centralizing self-attention ("I and my world"); and (3) the
elaboration of otherness. Buber had intended to clarify this in his
anthropology but never did so. "It seems to me I have made a little
discovery," he wrote in asking if I knew any books on the subject,
"but it is not easy to express it."

Phillips's rejection of "Hope for This Hour" reminded me of
Whitehead's fallacy of the misplaced concrete. When I acknowledged Phillips's letter, I remarked that Buber would undoubtedly say that the real concrete is relation between men and social

movements understood in terms of those relations themselves. Still, the prestige of "objectification" in the social sciences, I argued, was overpowering.

At about this time, I felt a responsibility, even amid my translating Buber's work, to write a novel about my experience with the psychodrama group I had briefly joined during my time in the civilian service. When I told my friend and colleague Alan Skelly about this, he seemed disturbed about the idea, telling me that no great communication is personal or autobiographical. I felt that I must be autobiographical to be concrete. The events alone could not convey the superpersonal meaning I saw in them, but my perspective of distance from them and a new relation with them, I thought, would do so. "I do not understand what your friend means by saying that no great communication is personal or autobiographical," Buber replied when I told him of Skelly's response. "Some of the greatest are, to begin with, Plato's *Seventh Epistle* and to end with Kierkegaard's *Point of View for My Activity as Author*. You should write the novel indeed." This comment, I replied, was "heartening to me as also your statement that I should write the novel. It is something I feel a responsibility to do without knowing whether I am capable of doing it or how I shall find time to do it."

My friendship with Abraham Joshua Heschel at this time made me quite anxious. Heschel very much wanted me to begin being an observant, practicing Jew. I wrote to Buber requesting advice on the matter of observing Jewish ritual and law, as much to better understand Buber's views on the question as to work through my personal conflict about befriending these two men, immersing myself in the dialogical theory of Hasidic Judaism, on the one hand, and on the other in the views of one who saw observation of Jewish custom as imperative to practicing Judaism. "I feel further than ever from traditional Judaism, as it is symbolized in Orthodox, Conservative, and even Reform temples as they are found in this country," I told Buber once.

There is little to be hoped. Yet I am sometimes troubled by the absence of any set of extensive religious observance in my own life. This trouble comes from my previous period of mysticism when religious practice was a central part of life as well as from the insistence of Dr. Heschel that one can only understand Judaism by taking part in it, that *kavana* does not come by itself apart from daily prayer.

I never felt fully at ease with the fact that I had not entered a specific spiritual practice. Dr. Heschel often questioned this from the standpoint of the need for community and prayer, the need to be filled with *kavana* but not to be set aside till *kavana* comes.

Buber replied, characteristically, that he could not see a problem like this independently of his personal experience. "For me," Buber wrote, "I know that I try to do what I experience I am ordered to do." Buber continued:

How can I make this into a general rule about ritual being right or wrong and so on? I open my heart to the Law to such an extent that if I feel a commandment being addressed to me I feel myself bound to do it as far as I am addressed—for instance, I cannot live on Sabbath as on other days, my spiritual and physical attitude is changed, but I have no impulse at all to observe the minutiae of the *Halakha* about what work is allowed and what not. In certain moments, some of them rather regular, some other just occurring, I am in need of prayer and then I pray, alone of course, and say what I want to say, sometimes without words at all, and sometimes a remembered verse helps me in an extraordinary situation; but there have been days when I felt myself compelled to enter into the prayer of a community, and so I did it. This is my way of life, and one may call it religious anarchy if he likes. . . . I cannot say anything but, put yourself in relation as you can and when you can, do your best to persevere in relation, and do not be afraid!

Understanding that my work was driven not just by the search for a vocation but also by a deeper, personal need for meaning, Buber also told me that my "urgent need can be satisfied only by something you will do and not by something you will receive." Suggesting the profound wholeness he saw in work done in the right spirit, Buber advised that "such a task cannot be given you but by the whole life you have lived until now. If I had known you for some time, I would probably be able to tell whether it should be teaching or writing, but I am inclined to think it is writing," he said, even as my journey of committed teaching at Sarah Lawrence was underway. "At any event, the task I assume is meant for you in this hour is to write a chapter (not at all an autobiographical one!) in the phenomenology and history, let us say in the historical phenomenology, of Doubt. Doubt, as you certainly know, is one of the most important factors in the development of faith." Suggesting his own philosophy of writing, he wrote that in this chapter on Doubt, I "must avoid all general terms. Relate as exactly and formulate as precisely as possible. The great enemy of such a work is vagueness. But I think you know this too," he added. At this time, however, I was still working to keep pace with integrating Buber's continued output, and my continued translating of it, into *The Life of Dialogue*, which evolved as Buber wrote and as our exchange continued.

Buber had, at this time, no plans to return to America any time soon. He wrote that his last tour was exhausting and that he had just now, at the end of 1952, begun to recover from it. Instead, wishing to visit with Buber again, I decided to try to receive a grant to go to Jerusalem. Eugenia and I started a class in oral Hebrew at the Young Men's Hebrew Association so that we could learn enough to come to Israel and work "in a year or two." Buber's lengthy reply expressed characteristic concern for our well-being: Would we know enough Hebrew? Would the funding be sufficient for the two of us? What was I planning to write to the Hebrew University to receive funding for my visit?

Buber, in the meantime, received what he called "a very queer letter from a German paper editor, whom I do not know personally (maybe I met him many years ago) and whom I would think mad," who suggested that Buber himself should "be put at the head of Germany." "Curiously enough," Buber wrote, this editor had "chosen two men"—himself along with Albert Schweitzer, "who are not German," as ideal presidents for Germany. "Of course," Buber added, "I would not accept even an unanimous vote." Like Buber, I was suspicious of the tendency of electoral politics to entrench the "I-It" spirit. During the closing weeks of the presidential campaign in the United States, it seemed to me, "people were much more engaged in seeing through and unmasking than in hearing the other side." Engaging the problem of dialogue in real politics, Buber presented his lecture on "The Validity and Limits of the Political Principle" to seven German universities the next year. "In Göttingen," he told me, "many hundreds of students assembled after the lecture before the university in an ovation."

Part of my concern with political life had to do with the difference between "Being and Seeming" as Buber treated it in "Elements of the Interhuman," which addressed the meeting point between the false social confirmation that does not have regard for a person's real fulfillment of his unique created goal and the true confirmation that does. Even presumably honest men resort to appearance on many social occasions and, far more often than they may be aware of, care about what others think and act and speak in anticipation of how they will seem to others. Accepting the direction toward which Buber points—an authentic life between men that has overcome appearance—I also believed that the reasons why we seek false confirmation and resort to appearance go deep into the nature of society itself. As Buber wrote, the tendency toward appearance *"hat ihrer Ursprung in der Rueckseite des Zwischenmenschlichen selber in der Abhängigkeit der Menschen voneinander"* (has its origin in the reverse side of the interhuman itself, in the dependence of human beings on one another).

To Buber, I expanded this statement in the following way: (1) The tendency toward appearance has its origin partly in ordinary amenities of civilized life—the politeness that makes us habitually pretend toward others what we do not feel; (2) in the institutionalization of social life that makes us relate toward others in terms of their function and in terms of their and our relative positions in these institutions; (3) in the tremendous emphasis on prestige and authority that is a corollary of these institutions; (4) in our inner divisions, which make us unable to relate to others honestly because we cannot relate as a whole; and (5) in our great weakness and our tremendous need of one another that makes most people unable to dispense with the confirmation of others, even if it's false, and unaware of the extent to which their values and attitudes do, in fact, arise not from a genuine relation to truth but from the social attitudes of the groups to which they feel themselves tied and from which they are unable to separate themselves because of insufficient strength (or confirmation) in themselves. I felt that one must to some extent become aware of and wrestle with this hidden social rootedness if one is to overcome appearance.

As I neared the completion of *The Life of Dialogue*, meanwhile, my old interest in mysticism and Eastern spirituality continued, though modified by Buber's critique of spiritualism. I had, in late 1952, gone to hear the scholar Gerald Heard, who spoke to me of his meeting with Buber. Two important mystics I met after their lectures, Swami Nikhilananda of the Ramakrishna-Vivekananda and D. T. Suzuki, also spoke favorably of their earlier encounters with Buber. I had begun reading Suzuki's *Essence of Buddhism* and was, I confessed to Buber, "very struck by its resemblance to your thought in his insistence on paradox and his refusal of the dualism between the sense world and the world of the spirit. This dualism," I thought, "clearly seemed to underlie the Vedanta and Swami Nikhilananda's 'non-dualism.'" True to form, Buber was critical of mystical worldviews, though engaged in understanding them. "As to mysticism," Buber replied to my letter expressing an ongoing interest in the connection between mysticism and his thought, "I thought I had made my attitude to it so clear in the Buddha chapter of *I and Thou* that I could stress this time the truly religious element (devotion of the whole person to the transcendence) to be found even in some so-called pantheists (Spinoza was a pantheist) and even in Gautama himself, without the risk of being misunderstood." As it was expressed in Christianity, mysticism had become a "pretension of the Church to be the realization of the biblical concept of the living human body—the people in its corporeal existence—a pretension based on the supposition of Israel being rejected by God." This pretension on the part of the Church "meant and means giving up the biblical fullness of the concept, the unity of body and spirit, replacing the body-element by the spiritual *corpus Christi*," an abstract concept that both misappropriated the meaning of spiritual fullness in community and elided the centrality of dialogue in Hebrew tradition.

The year 1952 also saw the beginning of fruitful conversations among myself, Buber, and scholars whose role in Buber's philosophical history would become pivotal. The 1957 Carl Rogers–Martin Buber dialogue, in which Buber would differ from Rogers on several important aspects of dialogue and insist upon what he called the "normative limitation of mutuality"—that is, limitations on genuine dialogue impressed by professional relationships such as that between a therapist and a patient—was instigated by a conversation in letters between Rogers and myself.

After sending me some as yet unpublished essays of Rogers's and my writing about them in reply, Rogers wrote to me that "I am very favorably impressed with your summary of my point of view. I believe it a more accurate picture than most psychologists would give." I would, as a result, end up moderating the Buber-Rogers conversation. "Rogers's unpublished papers impress me by their simplicity, honesty, and genuine open-mindedness," I told Buber. "This makes it all the more important that he is moving in your direction," which I believed that he was. At the time, as Rogers himself admitted, his philosophy was closer to Kierkegaard than to Buber in that he held to the impossibility of real communication, and hence the difficulty of effective teaching. His emphasis, following the existentialist train of thought, was more on the *subject* than on the "between," though he was beginning to acknowledge the latter. "Real communication," Buber held, "is not possible on the basis of Kierkegaard's kind of relationship to men. With men you cannot communicate really without being present *Vergegenwaertigung*, only with God can you be without it."

Wishing to build a bridge between Kierkegaard and Buber, however, a young scholar Mitchell Bedford wrote to me wishing "to contrast and compare the writings, teachings, and biographies of Soren Kierkegaard and MB. 'He is obviously a Freudian,' I told Buber, 'as he is writing about "mothers." Why those people think infancy more influential on ideas than youth,' I added, 'I cannot understand.'" Buber registered his distaste for Freudian theory in his reply, stating that Mitchell was "possessed by 'analysis' and probably cannot be saved from it for the time being." In all likelihood, Buber confided, "most psychoanalysts, knowing me to be an 'adversary,' will deny having learned anything from me." Both Rogers and Bedford did go on to learn much from Buber, and he from them, over the years.

By March 1953, I wrote to Buber that "I have finally finished my book *Martin Buber: The Life of Dialogue*." This was only partially true. The book, as Buber confirmed, still needed cutting before it could find a press. "Although the pressure of trying to complete it while performing other duties has caused me great anxiety," I confessed, "I have never lost sight of the extra dimension of meaning that your thought has added to my life, and for this I shall always be grateful to you and for that grace that brought me into relation with you." Professor Arnold Bergstrasser, the chair of my doctoral committee, was interested in seeing my book published, and was, in his words, "anxious to have it done by the University of Chicago Press" since there was "no adequate introduction to the work of Martin Buber in America" and such an introduction was "needed the more the farther reaching Buber's impact turns out to be in Europe." In August 1953, Bergstrasser visited Buber in Germany, and by the end of the year I had received notice from the University of Chicago Press saying that the Board of Publications had accepted my book. Before the book would go to press, however, Buber urged me to not write about his wife, Paula. "My wife," he said, "does not like at all that people write about her person." Paula Buber had written short stories and two epic novels under the pseudonym Georg Munk, and Buber's great friend Gustav Landauer had once seriously offended her by revealing at a social gathering that she was the pseudonymous author.

Soon after I completed my initial draft of *The Life of Dialogue*, Harold Taylor, president of Sarah Lawrence College, renewed my teaching contract, saying that none of the new teachers had the dedication that I had in working with students and that this was decisive in the college's decision. As my academic career moved forward, Buber offered advice that I took to heart. I was concerned, at the time my contract was renewed, that I was placing too much importance on financial security and that somehow this would interfere with more important interests. When I expressed this concern, Buber wrote, "I want to tell you that I am not in principle opposed to 'security,' especially in view of a child to come; what I am opposed to is sacrificing the very meaning of life (not less than that) to security." The great problem for me was one of when hanging on to security threatens the meaning of life and when it does not and also of ascertaining when giving up security itself directly threatens the meaning of life. I am not the first, and certainly will not be the last, scholar to navigate this difficult early-career dilemma. However, I loved teaching, and drew a good deal of my life's meaning from that vocation. Eugenia had recently accepted a leadership role at a synagogue nursery school after only three months of teaching there, which meant both that we would have to move out to a suburb of Manhattan in the fall and also that we would not plan to have a child any time soon.

It was Buber's view that I was packing too much into my course at Sarah Lawrence College, another problem known to haunt young academics. "You cannot do real work without self-limitation," he wrote, and he was "rather terrified" when he thought of my pupils being demanded to grasp all that I was throwing at them. "I remember I needed once a whole course to explain" just a few "selected chapters of the *Tao Te Ching* to a rather distinguished audience of university teachers, physicians, etc.," Buber wrote, referring to a series of lectures he had given in the Netherlands in 1924, which had been attended by Carl Jung's wife Emma and Hans Trüb, among others. As to Buber's teaching, the senate of the Hebrew University conferred upon him an honorary doctorate in 1953, which till then had been conferred only on Einstein, Chaim Weizmann, who coworked with Buber in the Democratic Faction of the Zionist movement in their youth and was first president of the new State of Israel, and Judah Magnes, first president and chancellor of the Hebrew University of Jerusalem and coworker with Buber for Jewish-Arab rapprochement. Later that year, I was writing to Buber to congratulate him on receiving the German publisher's Peace Prize, adding, "I know that you are the only person who could embody the meeting of the German and the Jewish people" and I felt that he was "being awarded the Peace Prize not in spite of but because of your dialogue (your Gegenueberstehen) with Germany." "It makes me happy," I told him, "that you are coming so much into your own in Europe and particularly in Germany," which obviously had "great symbolic value."

Buber and I were both astonished when Trude Rosmarin, editor of the *Jewish Spectator*, accused Buber of "creeping to the cross" because the ceremony at which he was awarded the German Book Trade Peace Prize was held in Paulskirche, a building in Frankfurt that had long ago ceased to be a church and that was chosen for the ceremony because of its historical character. The German revolutionary parliament of 1848 assembled there and since then it had become a kind of universalist symbol of antichauvinist democracy. The former two prizes, awarded in 1951 to Albert Schweitzer and in 1952 to Romano Guardini, were also given there, and the location had become part of the tradition. When the Yiddish press received a copy of Buber's speech, which included a serious condemnation of German behavior under the Nazi regime, a writer for *Der Tag* wrote that Buber was the only Jew who ever spoke so directly to the Germans about their actions. Albert Dann wrote to Buber from Sussex, England, that he was particularly pleased that Buber had spoken such *"weltverbindende"* [world-uniting] words in the Paulskirche because his grandfather—Rabbi Dr. Leopold Stein—had spoken similar words for peace a century earlier at a rabbinical conference in the same place. No one who reads Buber's speech on receiving the Peace Prize of the German Book Trade, I believed then and still believe today, could accuse him of forgetting the Jewish people in accepting the prize. And I never have yet seen the distinction between the responsibilities of different groups within one people so finely, concretely, and realistically drawn.

While I was hard at work revising and cutting *The Life of Dialogue*, with Eugenia's invaluable help, I accepted a position at a

Conservative synagogue in White Plains, New York, teaching a post–bar mitzvah, pre-confirmation class. I liked the idea of taking part in Jewish education if I did not have to pretend to be observant and did not have to espouse the dogmas of Conservative Judaism, but I was terrified at what I had undertaken—keeping thirteen- and fourteen-year-olds in line and reaching them at their level. The mother of one of my pupils, a pianist and composer from Frankfurt, Germany, contrasted Frankfurt's education with the failure of American teachers to expect serious study from their students. Sadly, I quit in the middle of the year because the pupils showed even less respect for their teachers than they did in the public schools.

Buber went over each of the chapters of *The Life of Dialogue* as I was revising it, making suggestions and keeping me abreast of his ever-growing bibliography. In this sense, the book, as with my translations of Buber, was the product of a dialogue between us. A friend once said to me, around this time, "Friedman and Buber are one," that it was not as if one were reading about one man writing about another. I much preferred this kind of statement to those who, not understanding Buber, criticized me for not criticizing him, for not imitating their own critiques. I felt then, and still feel, as I told Buber, "that the first function of the interpretative scholar is to understand, clarify, systematize, and evaluate, into which adverse criticism may or may not come depending upon the attitude of the scholar in question." Giving it the intensity and concentration that Buber prescribed in advising me on *The Life of Dialogue*, I was never bored!

7

Personal Direction

Letters, 1954–1957

In May 1954 I received a letter from Dr. Heinz Joachim Heydorn, who had written a fine article on Buber as a Socialist, in which he asserted that next to Albert Schweitzer Buber stood out as the person with the greatest integrity in the world at the time. In his words, referring to Buber's collection of Hasidic tales *The Legend of the Baal Shem*, which Buber had just then been correcting and revising, he wrote that Buber's Hasidic writings have created something splendid from the heritage of the Polish Jews; it is a treasure that will last as long as men ask the greatest questions of human life.

On sending me a corrected version of *The Legend of the Baal Shem* several months later, Buber's view of the work was more circumspect. "It has improved very much," he wrote, "more than I had hoped it would. But it has been a terrible piece of work. I was rather shocked by the pathetic lightheartedness of my youth. And you maybe are shocked by my cruel shortenings! But you will understand later on I have been right" in editing the book.

As Buber put the finishing touches on his collection of Hasidic tales, the problem of my personal direction came forcibly to the fore. My position as a member of both the social sciences and literature faculties, teaching hybrid courses in philosophy and literature (with titles such as "The Image of Man in Modern

Literature," "Religion and Philosophy," and "Philosophy through Literature"), was symbolic, I felt, of my inability to concentrate in any one of these three fields and of my need to hold on to my own center rather than fit into traditional classifications. I found that even at a progressive college like Sarah Lawrence people wanted me to be either a philosopher or a teacher of literature, but not both. I was impressed by Buber's personal and professional guidance as I navigated these disciplinary questions, especially his advice to concentrate on literature in the interest of concreteness, since losing contact with concrete reality undermined the very justification of philosophy.

As ever, my personal and professional searching overlapped, and I continued to press Buber on the place of mysticism and meditation in spiritual life. For Buber, Hasidism was in general not mystical in the sense that it sought mystical unity, but it was mystical in the sense that it aimed toward *ekstasis* in and through dialogue. As long as *unio mystica*, or mystical union, was not the aim of mysticism, Buber had no objection to it, but what Buber did not like were ambiguous terms that pointed to abstract ends. Being addressed by a situation and called to respond in the fullness of I-Thou was, Buber felt, something exceptional. It required a particular daring, but nothing more, no trappings of transcendence. For Buber, who had, like myself, delved into contemplative spirituality during World War II, the problem with mysticism was that it required willed "pre-meditated" meditations. "As to meditations coming spontaneously," he told me, "I knew them in earlier days, but never since my thought reached its maturity. What came in their place is something very different, something always bound to a reality, to a situation. I cannot but think all this talk about meditations rather exaggerated," he concluded.

> The essential trait of mysticism [Buber wrote to me], was the belief in a (momentous) union with the divine or the absolute,

a union occurring not after death but in the course of mortal life, as an interruption. If you read attentively the introduction to *Ekstatische Konfessionen*, you will see that even then, in my "mystical" period, I did not believe in it, but only in a "mystical" unification of the Self, identifying the depth of the individual self with the Self itself. Perhaps the main point in my personal evolution was the rejection of this mysticism.

Since the term "mysticism" had become "more nebulous" since the days of his youth, Buber did "not like to use it without explaining thoroughly what I mean and what not":

> Of course you may call it so if something is "told" me through a situation; I do not call it so, because this "being told" is simply the minimum of revelation, the elemental form of universal revelation, and revelation has nothing to do with mysticism. As for "meditation," as far as I see, people mean by it absorption in the absolute Self, more or less by the "inner" way; this is distant from what I mean as the religious attitude.

This distinction between mysticism and revelation, between being addressed and addressing and becoming a Self, ran through Buber's work, as it did through his constant suggestions to me that, in my work and personal life, I concentrate on that which comes to meet me concretely.

Nonetheless, I still felt there was something mystical in Hasidic practice. In addition to the communal life and the "sanctification of the everyday" in Hasidism, I saw an individual mysticism closer to that of other religions, particularly devotional Christianity. Buber had, after all, spoken of Hasidism as the movement in which revelation and mysticism, tradition and the timeless meet. He had written to me, "Revelation has nothing to do with mysticism." But if revelation is universal, is not mysticism also part of it? While the I-Thou relationship does not mean turning within, it seemed nonetheless to have many of the same qualities of presentness and ineffability as mysticism. Moses at the burning bush, for example, received not only the tradition—the God of the fathers—but also the presentness (and continuing presentness) of God's statement "I shall be there as I shall be there." It seemed to me that what distinguished Buber's use of the I-Thou from most Christian theologians was that he did not accentuate the transcendence of the Thou at the expense of a God who is "Nearer to me than myself," but that he saw both in a non-logical, non-theological manner that seemed to have roots in his earlier mystical phase.

As Buber and I engaged these questions, I had been learning a great deal teaching at a Conservative Sunday school, but I did not learn quite what I expected. If things had been different, I might have learned how to put on *tefillin* (I saw the boys in the group do it several times) and also learned prayers and other essential parts of the Jewish tradition. Mostly, however, I learned about the inner workings of a million-dollar synagogue; the absence of communication between the rabbi, the director of the religious school, and the religious school committee; the discrepancy between stated and actual purposes; and the externally oriented attitude toward ritual, tradition, and religious issues. Whatever our heady discussions yielded, my personal experience of ritual Judaism merely underscored the intensity of the challenge that Buber's philosophy of I-Thou posed to religious people everywhere.

Somewhat oddly, perhaps, while I saw the value of Martin Buber's *I and Thou* to religious people, neither Buber nor I wished to see it become a particularly popular book. When I told Buber, in the middle of 1954, of a man who approached me shortly after I started teaching at the New School for Social Research in New York City (where I taught for twelve years) with a rather grandiose scheme for granting scholarships in Buber's name to those who best understood *I and Thou* as a way of popularizing the book, Buber found the idea "rather strange." "*I and Thou* cannot—and shall not—become a popular book," he wrote. Like Buber, I did not see the idea as at all practical or valuable. When I stressed how much work and devotion it had taken me to write my book about Buber and that I did not want this scheme to interfere with that in any way, the young man finally agreed to desist. Buber wrote me that the plan seemed to him to represent the American business spirit, one that would make a profit out of a serious inquiry and, probably, dilute its immediate relevance at the same time. "I have an 'objective' aversion against the idealistic extravagances of the business spirit, especially if they try to involve me in their affairs," he wrote to me after describing his polite letter declining the idea. It seems, in retrospect, that Buber's reluctance to see *I and Thou* overly popularized may have been commensurate with his understanding of religious action. "Religion," Buber wrote to me in 1955, "must transfuse itself into the whole life of the person, including its full activity." To separate out the I-Thou relation from the wholeness of religious activity would be to remove from the life of dialogue the context of religious community in which it was grounded. It could become, as in some respects it has, pop philosophy with no relation to the full religious life of men and women.

In the summer of 1955, meanwhile, I taught a course in contemporary religious thought for the Department of Religion at Columbia University. The success of this course led Professor Horace Friess of the Department of Religion to think of me as a possible regular faculty member of the department. Sometime in 1956, I was considered for the position along with Jacob Taubes, who was finally appointed. My dear friend Professor Abraham Joshua Heschel of the Jewish Theological Seminary said he would use his influence to help me attain the position if I would embark on what he called "the holy dimension of Jewish deeds"; that is, if I would begin to follow *Halakhah*. Although I knew that Heschel wanted only a beginning, not a total commitment, and that he felt that "a little with *kavana* was better than much without," I could not bring myself to say that I would do as he wished. As a result, he did not help me find a position, though he never cut off our friendship and professional relationship.

Buber agreed to write a letter recommending me to the position at Columbia, for which I remain eternally grateful. "I am going to tell you what I think of Maurice Friedman," he wrote to the chair of the Department of Religion at Columbia. "I do so at his request, but I rather like doing it," he added, continuing:

> I have learned to know what kind of man he is, just by seeing, in the course of about five years, how he works. The work I am alluding to interested me first because my own thought was its subject, but soon I was attracted by his way of working. He began by having a clear-cut idea of what he wanted to make, and then he devoted himself to it. He concentrated on the matter the power of his mind, a brave lot of powers, and he went on without flinching. Now I must tell you, it was not an easy job. He had to gather a mass of stuff, to coordinate it, and to build up something like a system out of what was never intended to become such a thing. This he could do only by true understanding, his best quality indeed. He understands the ideas he meets, and he understands even the persons who thought them, as persons who thought just these ideas and not different ones. I am sorry to say that he had to do in this case with a somewhat resisting subject, but he succeeded to grasp it adequately. His best faculty is to express and to explain what he has understood. . . . I have the impression that I have told you what perhaps no other could tell you about the man. It is because for all these years I have been a witness and now I have come to give evidence.

Buber's letter pleased me in particular because its emphasis on my ability to understand the persons I studied *as persons* contrasted with his response six years earlier to my long written account of my life when he said that I showed only my feeling about the persons I told about and did not enable the reader to imagine them as themselves. I credit my engagement with Buber himself, both the man and his philosophy, to this personal development.

Of *The Life of Dialogue*, Buber had written, "To systematize a wild-grown thought as mine without impairing its elementary character seems to me a remarkable achievement. On a rather multifarious work Friedman has not imposed an artificial unity, he has disclosed the hidden one."

Buber's advice to me, when it came to navigating the politics of academia, helped me to navigate disappointments and potential conflicts and might stand as advice to academics of any era. In the mid-1950s, a number of internal struggles emerged at Sarah Lawrence centering around the president of the college, Harold Taylor. "I would like to advise you," Buber wrote in response to my letters explaining the situation, "to remain in it as long as you are able to without being affected too much by what is going on. This is a great chance to get a real experience of right and wrong elements in what we call democracy and even to learn to distinguish between right and wrong democracy, something you can acquire by experience only, and especially by experience in a nonpolitical institution."

A minor difference of opinion between Buber and the great theologian Reinhold Niebuhr suggested the way Buber believed one should comport oneself in the face of attempts to politicize philosophy and theology, especially when politics involved personally attacking a writer and thinker for perceived shortcomings. In a review of *The Life of Dialogue* for the *New York Times*, in which he argued, among other things, that Buber was "antipolitical," Niebuhr had taken exception to a statement by Hans Heydorn that "next to Schweitzer Buber is the symbol of integrity." For evidence to the contrary, Niebuhr drew on what he viewed as Schweitzer's unacceptable treatment of the Africans he came into contact with. "What you tell me about the judgment Niebuhr passed on Schweitzer," Buber wrote, "is incomprehensible. I have known Schweitzer for very many years and never saw anything 'fake' in him. Of course, he is not a 'saint'—who is? But I believe him to be a true man." Buber's belief that even a limited person could stand as a "true man" was parallel to his belief that we should engage in dialogue beyond differences— as he had advised me to begin doing when I complained to him about the absurdity of people I had met during the war and as he had practiced in his attempt to reengage the German people. Further, he rejected out of hand the view that his work was anti-political, and he requested that I send Niebuhr his paper "The Validity and Limits of the Political Principle." "I have never been anti-political," he wrote to me, "neither in theory nor in practice, but I think it vitally important to fix the boundaries of politics, at least as long as it is not possible to put the power of decision in the hands of the best men (not 'the philosophers,' as Plato thought, but the best men indeed), a thing that would increase the tragedy in the life of those men but would diminish the tragedy in the life of mankind."

After reading his review of *The Life and Dialogue*, I wrote Neibuhr a letter that sparked a revealing conversation suggestive of the differences between Neibuhr's view of the relation between politics and dialogue and Buber's. My letter said little about Neibuhr's critique of Buber's politics. "What you have to say about Buber himself is as important as what you say about the book since many readers of the review must have been previously unfamiliar with Buber or unaware of his importance," I wrote. In spite of my and Buber's concern that his philosophy of I-Thou became watered down by overpopularization, I was always glad to see Buber's ideas reach the mainstream, since I believed in their importance for the fuller life of humankind.

Neibuhr replied that he must completely disagree with Buber on his attitude toward political problems since Buber makes the dialogical relation between person and person the absolute norm. While Buber called for a restructuring of society along somewhat socialistic lines that would make dialogical relations in general more accessible to men, Niebuhr found it ironic that Buber should be so personal, not to say individualistic. It was well known that Niebuhr regarded Hebrew thought as superior to Christian thought, because it is concerned with justice rather than love.

In reply, I wrote to Niebuhr a very long, probably too long, letter, which quoted, in part, from Buber himself: "Herberg, like Niebuhr, has not grasped why my 'social philosophy' is as it is: because I do not see any salvation, any true help coming from the non-personal. What they think practical is really the theory of a practice (just as Marx's philosophy) and never becomes real praxis, real act. What is done in the social field is done out of personal relation, out of *die Menge entmenten* (to decrowd the crowd).'" Genuine dialogue, Buber believed, could restore the personal to social relations. For Niebuhr, Buber's views did not emphasize enough what Niebuhr saw as the political necessity to encourage social justice, something which he believed could only be done collectively. Whereas Niebuhr argued that Buber did not have a sufficient instrument in the "I-Thou" relationship for dealing with the problem of justice, I asked whether the institutionalizing of sin in social and political institutions does not lead to an "Immoral Society" (which was the second half of the title of Niebuhr's most famous book *Moral Man and Immoral Society*).

What was particularly in question, as I told Niebuhr, was whether the highest value of the one sphere (love) can be carried over into the other sphere (justice). I quoted to Niebuhr from the "Social Philosophy" chapter in *The Life of Dialogue*, where I argued that "Relation is the true starting point for personal integration and wholeness and for the transformation of society, and these in turn make possible ever greater relation." However, "if the basic reality and value is the concrete dialogical relation between men, then there is a vital necessity for a restructuring of society that will enable the relation between men to be of a more genuinely dialogical nature." Niebuhr saw the political sphere as more of an independent reality and less amenable to the influence of the personally dialogical. Buber seemed to have more hope than Niebuhr that the values of direct relation may be carried over into politics, including political action as a member of a large-scale group. Several years later, in 1959, Buber would write that "I do not think the difference between my position and Niebuhr's is expressed by 'social vs. political.' Rather, he is interested in society as an institutional reality and I as a relational one (as far as built up on personal human relations)." This distinction fairly summarized the philosophical differences between Martin Buber and Reinhold Niebuhr.

For Buber, what Niebuhr called "the basic structure of society" was "historically and even pre-historically (this is my opinion against the prevailing opinion of ethnologists) based on personal relations, and when it subdues them it becomes wrong." In the "modern technical society" of the postwar years, the "artfully constructed equilibria of power" in the relation between nations depended upon the ordering of society "and not its justice." Buber believed that Niebuhr needed "to distinguish carefully between two very different kinds of 'justice,'" one social and personal and the other emerging from obedience to God's will. Buber found himself "harassed by the thought [that] the concept of justice must be split in two, bearing even different names. I cannot see the God-willed reality of justice anywhere," he wrote to me, other "than in being 'just,' and this means of course: being just as far as it is possible here and now, under the 'artful' conditions of actual society." Such a practice of justice could only emerge from relating dialogically to each situation as it occurred. In striving toward such a dialogical justice, "I go on in the dark, till my head meets the wall and aches, and then I know: Here is (now) the wall, and I cannot go further. But I could not know it beforehand." In other words, practicing "I-Thou" justice meant engaging the particular dialogical situation in order to discover the limits of justice in practice rather than walking a prelit path of justice conceived in theological abstraction. The social structure and its attendant philosophies of being might not change, but the limits of justice depended upon personal exploration in genuine meeting, not on the structures of society. Even such a cherished abstract idea as Freedom, Buber held, could only be enacted between person and person and was at best an "indispensable presupposition, it is no more than this and it should not be proclaimed as more." "The Americans," who cherish Freedom in the abstract as the main path to justice, Buber wrote to me once, "do not know what they lose by so doing." What they lost, and what all abstractions lost, was the primacy of the personal relation.

Practically speaking, Buber's experience of the political life of the Jewish people in Israel was, of course, influenced by his sense of the need for dialogical relation. Buber always resisted too firm an attachment to ideology. In 1956, for instance, Joseph Ben-David came to America from Israel and organized the American Friends of Ihud, a leading organization, at the time, for Jewish-Arab rapprochement led by Judah Magnes and Buber and including Ernst Simon, Hugo Bergman, Chaim Kalvarisky, and others. I became president of the American Friends of Ihud and Ben-David was Secretary. We came into conflict over the tendency of Ben-David, Don Peretz, and others to use our organization to propagate anti-Zionism in American. Later I resigned over this issue, and Peretz, the vice president, rushed with the news to the executive council that I had naively imagined that by resigning I could raise a basic issue; in my stead, he had himself elected president. Although Ernst Simon later reproached me for resigning, two months later,

Ihud in Israel demanded that the American organization no longer use its name because it did not mirror faithfully the Zionism of the parent organization. For Buber, while Ben-David was "an honest man," he was "a radical ideologist, who does not see the reality" of the Palestinian-Israeli conflict "and consequently does not know how to deal with it." Rather than working to further dialogue between Zionists, who were not likely to change their views, anyhow, and Palestinians, who were equally entrenched, Ben-David's wing of Ihud sought to form an anti-Zionist political party. Ideological politics, Buber believed, would not address the situation and they were a distraction from the mission of Ihud and its friends in America, which was to further dialogue between these groups.

Indeed, our generation had witnessed the fallout of ideological struggle on many fronts. The death of Albert Einstein in April 1955 moved Buber deeply, and Buber later told me that Einstein refused an operation that would have saved his life because he was so depressed over the American use of the atomic bomb, which Einstein had been involved in helping to create. Politics, indeed, as Buber held, needed a boundary set between itself and the life of the mind and spirit!

Sometime around 1955 or 1956, I was asked to write a popular article on Buber for a short-lived journal, *Faith Today*. Buber's disciple Ernst Simon wisely remarked to me that this would be harder to do than my book on Buber. To help me in this project Buber sent me "an authentic anecdote" inscribed "For Maurice and Eugenia."

In May 1914, the old Rev. William Hechler (a helper of Zionism, because the Jews must be gathered together in Palestine before the Paraclete [the second coming of Christ] appears), whom I had not met for many years, came to see me in Zehlendorf, a suburb of Berlin. The first words he said were: "I have come to tell you that in this year the world war (a word I had not heard till then) will break out." He explained that it is foretold in the prophecy of Daniel. When he left after some hours, I accompanied him to the station. On the way he stopped and said: "My dear friend, we are living in einer grossen Zeit [in a great time]—tell me, please, do you believe in God?" I answered approximately: "No need to be concerned," meaning: Everything is in order. But when returning home alone, I asked myself: "Have I said the truth?" Did he not mean by "believing" something different from what I mean by it? Should I not have answered him: "If to believe in God means to be able to speak about him in the third person, I do not believe"? And I was grieved. But after some moments it came over me: "I am able to speak to God in the second person—is it not enough?!" Belief, so necessary to the life of dialogue, could not intervene, without effort in affirming the other, in the affairs and decisions of men of politics.

Indeed, the association between Israel and the pursuit of Jewish theology in religious studies was then weighing on my mind. In 1956, I picked up a post as visiting professor of religious philosophy at the Hebrew Union College in Cincinnati, which trains rabbis for the Reform Judaism movement. I was troubled, once again, with a professional question that impinged, as all professional questions do, on the personal and the political. I had made a good impression in Cincinnati, and was then considering a permanent position there. Buber's reply suggested the personal difficulty he himself experienced as one of Israel's unofficial ambassadors to the world. "If you want seriously ('existentially') to act educationally for the poor (very poor!) cause of Judaism," he told me, "you will decide to go to Cincinnati taking on yourself a lot of anger, disillusion and conflict. I would not even advise you to do so if you do not fully realize that it is so, and if you do not feel your heart strong enough to meet even the rather important petty contrarieties of everyday that await you in that ambiance—strong enough and loving enough." Such everyday contrarieties had dogged Buber for many years, but, for Buber, it was "only a question of love, involving love for the unlovable. If you do not feel this strength and this love, you will not be happy there," Buber advised. He was also concerned about Eugenia, who "must in some measure, so far as possible make that miserable cause her own."

My adventures in publishing with Buber continued apace as I weighed this decision carefully in my mind, finally deciding, for the second time in my life, to forgo an academic association with official Judaism in America. Walter Goldstein, who had written several books about Buber and Sartre, was upset when Routledge & Kegan Paul (my British publisher, thanks to Sir Herbert Read, who was on its board of directors and was very much into Buber) publicized *Martin Buber: The Life of Dialogue* as the first comprehensive book about Buber's thought. Goldstein felt that his books were already that. Buber advised that I "need not worry" since Goldstein was "a very unhappy man" who was nearly blind with illness and had suffered many misfortunes. But Buber did not elaborate.

That same year, Marc Chagall told me he had received a letter from Rayburn, the publisher of Buber's *Tales of Rabbi Nachman*, which I translated, but Chagall did not elaborate on the contents of the letter. I suspect Rayburn was requesting illustrations for one of Buber's books, possibly *The Tales of the Hasidim*, since Chagall's daughter had wanted Buber to ask Chagall to make illustrations to *The Tales*, which Buber did not want to do. "He is a very remarkable artist, and his new illustrations to the Bible are beautiful," Buber wrote to me, "but I rather prefer the tales remain unillustrated. I appreciate Chagall highly," Buber continued, "but his 'Hasidism' and mine are different and should better not be mixed." These drawings, had they been made, would have no doubt have contributed a remarkable store to Judeo-Christian iconographic art at mid-century, though Buber's reluctance to have *The Tales* illustrated was, of course, respected.

Not that Buber did not take serious suggestions. As I was translating *Pointing the Way*, I was troubled about including "Elements of the Interhuman" in the collection. It was, I thought, a different genre, form, and length from the rest of the essays in the book. Buber accepted my advice and put "Elements of the Interhuman" into *The Knowledge of Man*, which I subtitled *The Philosophy of the Interhuman*. This was around the same time that Buber's lecture "What Is Common to All," an unpacking of Heraclitus as Buber saw him, met an enthusiasm stronger than ever in Munich. The Munich press compared the effect of the lecture with that of Schelling's Munich lectures.

In 1956 Buber began making plans for a second visit to America for a lecture tour that I looked forward to with anticipation. The primary purpose of his visit was to give lectures and seminars for the Washington School of Psychiatry, which I told Buber I thought was a "wonderful, a quite remarkable opportunity to bring your insights into contact with a serious and ever more important segment of psychological thought." I had a very good impression of the institute. It was not at all orthodox Freudian—something Buber and I both found very important—and scholars at the institute were comfortable both with his criticism of Freud and, more importantly, his concern for the wholeness of man. My new friend Leslie Farber was planning to a give a paper on "Martin Buber and Psychotherapy" to a large audience in Washington, and I was going to be a discussant along with Reuel Howe, a professor at Virginia Theological Seminary and author of the book *Man's Need and God's Answer*. Leslie, who later wrote a book titled *The Miracle of Dialogue*, which I considered a miracle in itself in a review I wrote of it, was planning to use I-Thou dialogue as a critique of all other psychological schools in his paper on "Buber and Psychotherapy" at a panel the following March. Leslie sent Buber a copy of his paper ahead of time, and suggested at one point that we write a book jointly on the subject, which never came to pass.

Buber's schedule made the trip somewhat of a burden on him. Even to write two new lectures in time for the seminars would be what he called "a tremendous exertion." Buber's age and health were also beginning to catch up to him, and citing concerns about his health, he suggested postponing the seminars. In addition to his formal lectures for the Washington School of Psychiatry, Buber was scheduled to lead seven seminars. "I must live from now on more 'economically,'" he told me, noting that he was consulting a physician. Nonetheless, Buber forged ahead, deciding to "take the matter of the unconscious into the seminars," as he told me early in 1957. The main problem, which he begged me not to relate to anyone, is he had been led by his thoughts about the unconscious "deep into the problem of body and soul and that I have not yet found the language necessary to express what I mean." He planned "to elucidate the problem in the seminar as simply and slowly as possible without giving answers needing a new terminology." It was during his second visit to America that Buber focused his lectures and seminars on the relationship between psychology and I-Thou philosophy, a subject on which he departed to varying degrees from some of the preeminent psychologists of the 1950s.

8

The Washington School
of Psychiatry and the
Buber-Rogers Dialogue

In the spring of 1957 Martin and Paula came for their second visit to America, acting on the invitation of my friend Leslie Farber, chairman of the faculty of the Washington School of Psychiatry. Buber's great concern before coming to the Washington School of Psychiatry, in addition to his health and the problem of delving into the topic of the unconscious without unduly complicating matters, was the question of the publication by the Washington School of the four lectures Buber was scheduled to deliver, which were organized around the broad field of philosophical anthropology. Buber wanted to retain these lectures as a part of the book he was writing on the subject. It was agreed, after some discussion, that these lectures would be published in an issue of *Psychiatry*, the journal of the school, which left Buber free to include them in the book to be published by Harper and George Allen & Unwin in Britain.

Meanwhile, Farber received a $25,000 grant for a movie to be made of the seminars. This was, of course, before the age in which the whole event might have been preserved on videotape much more cheaply and without fanfare. Farber was delighted with this. But when he wrote Buber about it, Buber rejected his plan, saying he had "a radical need for spontaneity," and this would not be possible if a movie was made of the proceedings. Leslie Farber, Eugenia, and I all traveled from Washington to New York to greet Buber when he arrived. At that first meeting, Farber, who was understandably attached to his movie plan, again raised the question with Buber. But Buber once again declined, saying, "In twenty-five years, people will not even know what I was talking about!"

Through exhaustive correspondence between Buber, Farber, and myself, four public lectures by Buber were planned under the title "What Can Philosophical Anthropology Contribute to Psychiatry?" Also planned was a seven-session seminar with thirty participants on the unconscious and dreams. Most of the participants were psychiatrists, but a handful of philosophers and theologians were also present. The lectures were given at the Washington Cathedral, which is Episcopalian, and the seminars at the chapter house of the Cathedral.

Buber's four formal lectures were widely attended and were a great success. They began with "Distance and Relation," a lecture that Buber at first did not consider including in the schedule because he thought that the concepts were too difficult for an American audience. He decided, however, that this essay was a necessary introduction to the series. The following lecture, "Elements of the Interhuman," was much more accessible and constituted the real heart of the lectures. Buber and I worked together almost sixteen hours to revise Ronald Gregor Smith's translation of Buber's German for this lecture. At one point, when I objected strongly to the way Smith had broken up Buber's long sentences, Buber turned to Eugenia, who attended all these sessions, and said, "Your husband is a very stubborn man." "You call me stubborn!" I exclaimed. Where Buber was stubborn about matters such as Jewish-Arab relations, I was stubborn about grammar! "What Is Common to All," the lecture that took off from Heraclitus's saying

"One should follow the common," was delivered in two sections, since it was quite long. It had enormous implications that Buber's hearers only dimly grasped (though his critique of Huxley and the users of mescaline was undoubtedly clear enough for an age when many intellectuals were still enthralled with "psychedelic" drugs). I tried to spell out those implications in my introductory essay to *The Knowledge of Man* and some of my own later books, including my feeling that Buber's essay, "Guilt and Guilt Feelings," cannot be understood except on the basis of "What Is Common to All."

In the lectures, Buber did just what he said he would do in his letters to me on the subject. He shared his thoughts on the unconscious slowly and clearly, advancing a radically new theory that the unconscious was really the storehouse from which both consciousness and the bodily sensations arose and were elaborated. The implications of this theory we all tried to spell out together in the seminars—that it would change the whole way of looking at therapy and certainly would radically change the way in which Freud and most psychiatrists and psychoanalysts looked at the unconscious. Buber also devoted a couple of seminar sessions to dreams.

The thirty psychoanalysts, philosophers, and theologians who gathered in the chapter house for the seminars all experienced a remarkable interchange and interaction that gave a whole new dimension and meaning to the word "dialogue." I took fairly complete notes on these seminar sessions, all except one which I did not attend (I was committed to lecturing at Vanderbilt University the one time I missed). When I wrote my introductory essay (Chapter 1) for Buber's anthropology book *The Knowledge of Man* (*A Philosophy of the Interhuman,* as I subtitled it), I suggested to Buber that I might include these notes in the section on the unconscious. He consented to my paraphrasing them, but not to my publishing the notes as such. Yet when Buber and his great friend the

German scholar Grete Schaeder put together his *Nachlese* ("Glean-ings," or *A Believing Humanism* in its American title), they asked me to send them my notes and had them translated into German for this book! When I translated *A Believing Humanism*, I did not, of course, retranslate my notes but simply copied them into it.

At one point in the seminars, Buber remarked, "My friend Maurice Friedman knows more about me than I do." I was not at all sure that this was a compliment as Buber was not very inter-ested in facts about himself!

At the beginning of the second seminar, I summarized what Buber had said to us in the first seminar: "The basic distinction between the physical and the psychic, though not clear cut, does not follow into the unconscious, which is non-phenomenological and prior to the split between psychic and physical. Freud's logical error, followed by all schools of psychoanalysis, places the uncon-scious within the person alone, and I would add now, following a specious either/or, assumes it is psychic rather than physical. Hence reality is seen as psychic rather than interhuman."

In the third seminar, I asked Buber, "Is the unconscious, instead of a psychic sphere within, a sphere which has *more* direct contact with and part in the interhuman than the psychic? If so, would notions such as introjection and projection be partially open to question on that ground?" To this, Buber replied:

> In certain crises of later childhood I feel that more decisive for-mation is going on than in infancy. Social and cosmic puberty is what I refer to, and not just to sexual puberty. . . . If the unconscious is that part of the existence of a person in which the realms of body and soul are not dissociated, then the rela-tionship between two persons would mean the relationship between two non-divided existences. Thus the highest moment of relation would be what we call the unconscious. But the unconscious should have, may have, will have more influence

in the interhuman than the conscious. For example, in shaking hands, if there is a real desire to be in touch, the contact is not bodily or psychic, but a unity of one and the other. The unconscious as such does not enter easily into action. I pronounce a word, you receive it—the unconscious has no such means at its disposition. The unconscious sometimes leads to a half-articulated exclamation which all the prepared words cannot express. The voice becomes the direct instrument of the unconscious in that case.

Later in the seminars, referring to the central place "confirmation" from person to person plays in Buber's thought as that which enables the inmost becoming of the unique person to take place, I asked: "Does your view of the unconscious and of therapy imply confirmation instead of observation and transference? Or do transference and confirmation complement or include each other?" Buber replied, "Confirmation does not replace transference, but if meeting"—what Hans Trüb and Buber called *Heilung aus der Begegnung*, or literally "healing through meeting"—"is the decisive factor, the other concepts would change too, in both their meaning and their dynamic." Confirmation of the Other, Buber held, "can be misunderstood as *static*. I meet another—I accept and confirm him as he now is. But confirming a person *as he is* is only the first step, for confirmation does not mean that I take his appearance at this moment as the person I want to confirm. I must take the other person in his dynamic existence, in his specific potentiality." The specific potentiality of the person who steps forward to meet us, which "in religious terms" we might call his creative purpose, "makes itself felt to me as that which I would most confirm."

Given the context of Buber's talk, his response led me to ask if there was a special kind of confirmation for therapy. "I am inclined to think," Buber replied, "that in the strongest illness manifesting itself in the life of a person the highest potentiality of this person is manifesting itself in negative form. The therapist can influence in a direct way the growing up of potentialities. Healing is not bringing up of the old, but of the new, not bringing up of zero, but counterbalancing with the positive." Earlier in the seminar, Buber had said, "There are two kinds of therapists, one who knows more or less consciously the kind of interpretation he will get and the other . . . who does not know. I am entirely on the side of the latter. . . . The usual therapist imposes himself on the patient without being aware of it. What I mean is the conscious liberation of the patient from the unconscious imposition of the therapist—leaving the patient really to himself and seeing what comes of it." Only by thus dropping preconceptions of individual outcomes and attentively avoiding the imposition of these outcomes on the patient could a therapist help to make the full potential of the patient manifest.

At one point during a break in the seminars David Rioch—a prominent member of the institute—said he was going to challenge Buber after the break. After the break, he asked Buber, "What can you say about God in healing?" Buber replied, "In that moment when the name of God is mentioned, most human circles break asunder as persons without knowing it." Buber responded further, adding, "In that moment the commonness of thinking—the fact of thinking together—is disrupted. The difference between the world with God and without is so enormous that discussion of God must divide people except in a group united by a common faith. People say 'God' without meaning reality, as a sublime convention of the cultured person."[1] In one sense, Buber's answer was an evasion, but for good reason: throughout his work, Buber refused to separate the presence of God from the presence of relation. To invoke God in the abstract was to invoke a useless and even damaging sense of personal and group difference, as the sordid history of institutional religion has time and again demonstrated. God, for Buber, was the reality of relation, not the mark of culture.

Some time later, Reinhold Niebuhr's wife Ursula told me that David Rioch had said to her that of all that Buber uttered in those seminars, his refusal to answer this question about God and therapy is what had impressed him most. It was no accident that a volume of the Library of Living Philosophers was given over to Buber's work whereas Kegley and Bretall's Library of Living Theology made a place for Paul Tillich. Although Tillich was a systematic thinker, as Buber was not, Tillich was a theologian who accepted certain theological postulates on faith, whereas Buber was no theologian but a philosopher who tested everything he spelled out philosophically by his own experience wherever possible. That is why in the Postscript to *I and Thou* Buber urges his readers to try to experience what he has written as their own.

While at the Washington School, Buber came to a lecture on Buddhism that I had presented for a course on comparative religion and psychiatry. His only comment on the lecture was practical: he thought that I should set quotations apart by saying them more slowly and with special emphasis. When Les Farber asked him if he had given lectures as long as this in his time, he answered, "Oh much more. Once when I was lecturing, I noticed that my friends in the front row were looking tired. I discovered to my astonishment that I had been lecturing for three hours."

Curious to see the psychiatrists in their daily work life, and to attend another set of panels, Buber and I drove together to Chestnut Lodge, where psychiatrists of the Washington School practiced direct therapy with schizophrenics, something that Freud held could not be done. On the way, I told Buber how an incompetent psychiatrist had once pronounced me a schizophrenic because I said that I had remained inwardly calm and collected during a convulsion. "I'm sorry, my dear," Buber exclaimed. "You have no talent for schizophrenia." Buber told me on this drive that he did not expect the importance accorded Freud to last beyond the century. "Freud, like Marx, was one of the great simplifiers," he said. Later, at one point in the seminars, Buber elaborated on this thought: "Freud did not speak explicitly of the psyche but of the 'psychoate,'" he said, but "he never defines it." As a great simplifier, Freud was "one who places a general concept in place of the ever-renewed investigation of reality. A new aspect of reality is treated by the simplificator as the solution of one of the riddles of being. Fifty years of psychotherapeutic thought have been based on this dangerous manner of thinking. Now this period is at an end," Buber pronounced hopefully.

Along the way, as Buber wished me a lot of experience editing as well as a long life, he said, poignantly, "I love life." This simple proclamation, I believe, holds a key to Buber's work, his ever-renewed attempt to affirm the living over the abstract.

At Chestnut Lodge, one of the psychiatrists presented a paper on a patient whom he thought would interest Buber because of her concern with mysticism. Buber's only comment was, "I do not see the line of therapy here." The great psychiatrist Frieda Fromm-Reichmann (who was the model for the psychiatrist in the book and movie *I Never Promised You a Rose Garden*) was present. Later, she went to see Buber alone and told him of some deep problems she was having because she was so well known. Buber advised her to take a vacation in a place where no one knew her. But, she confessed, she could not resist going to a place where people did know her!

Shortly after the lectures and seminars for the Washington School of Psychiatry, Buber went to the University of Michigan for a conference centered on his work. I rode there with Buber's granddaughter Judith Agassi, who said to me on our drive, in words almost identical to those her father might utter, as Buber's son Rafael pointed out, "I am Buber's granddaughter, but I am not his disciple." Many years later, she edited a book of Buber's speeches on psychiatry—a surprising action for one who was no disciple!

At the conference in Michigan, I met Staughton Lynd, the son of my colleague Helen Merrell Lynd at Sarah Lawrence College, who was, at that time, a leading young historian at Yale. Another person I met in Michigan was Kenneth Boulding, a distinguished Quaker economist and author of the famous *Naylor Sonnets* that I had memorized when I was an attendant at Pennhurst, an institute for the "feeble-minded," as they called it during the war. Boulding, always a creative person, made up wonderful poems and drew pictures during Buber's lectures and the panels centered on his I-Thou philosophy. What struck me most about Boulding was that this remarkable theologian-poet (who had written "But there is joy greater than joy can know through suffering on the far side of woe" and "May we not see paradox blaze into mystery!") said to me, "If it were not for Christ, I might believe that God was the devil!" I need not spell out how far this statement was from Buber's own faith and my own. I do not mean by this that we did not place Christ at the center of our faith, but that we were far removed from Boulding's attitude toward evil.

The high point of the University of Michigan conference was the "dialogue" between Martin Buber and Carl Rogers, a distinguished American psychologist. This dialogue was taped, much to the annoyance of Leslie Farber, who had insisted that Buber should give no other talks on psychology while in America under the auspices of the Washington School of Psychiatry. I moderated the discussion between the two men and occasionally suggested issues I believed were important. Some years later, I discovered that Rogers was intensely annoyed at my interrupting his dialogue with Buber. This dialogue was justly famous, for it raised many important issues, probably the central of which was the notion of the "normative limitation of mutuality," Buber's idea that because patients look to therapists as authorities from whom they can derive certain knowledge, their I-Thou mutuality would necessarily be limited. "I could have been much harder on him," Buber said to me after the discussion, referring to his feeling that Rogers did not adequately appreciate the normative limitation of mutuality. But Buber also said to me, "Because of the way Rogers brought himself to the meeting, it was a real dialogue." None of the 400 people present were allowed to ask any questions. As a result of this experience overall, Buber had me delete the last paragraph of "Elements of the Interhuman," in which he stated that it is not possible to have a real dialogue before an audience. The Buber-Rogers dialogue has been translated into German and Japanese, and two professors of speech communication—Kenneth Cissna and Rob Anderson—have written two volumes on it, both published by the State University of New York Press, though neither of them was present at the dialogue itself. In their first volume, Cissna and Anderson said they found ninety instances of what they called Buber's "rhetoric of cannot"!

Sometime during the spring of 1957, Buber gave a seminar on biblical faith at Columbia University. Reinhold Niebuhr attended, one of his arms paralyzed. Also in attendance was James Muilenberg, who had written a splendid essay on Buber and the Bible where he said that since the days of St. Paul no one had dealt so seriously with the relation between the Judaism of the time of the New Testament and the Christianity of that time. In this seminar, Buber treated passages from the New Testament as well as from the Hebrew Bible. One particular passage that stands out in my memory is the one in the New Testament that says, "Since the days of John the Baptist people have tried to take the kingdom of heaven by force." Buber gave us an unusual interpretation of this passage, the details of which are not as interesting, in retrospect, as his response to several young scholars present to whom he gave his source for this interpretation, saying only that to them it seemed "subjective." After they pressed Buber, he finally said, "I do not hear the voice of Jesus in it." I knew that he felt that he really did hear the voice of Jesus, of Plato, and of certain other figures when he read them. But he urged me not to talk about this lest people think he was into some sort of extrasensory perception. After Buber had said this, James Muilenberg pounded the table and said, "That is pure subjectivity!" "I told you it was subjective," said Buber mildly.

Another person who attended this seminar was my Sarah Lawrence colleague Joseph Campbell, who was already well known through his book *The Hero with a Thousand Faces*, but not nearly as well known as he became posthumously after Bill Moyers released the series of tapes he made of his interviews with Campbell. To Campbell, all religions were essentially one, or should be, and could be boiled down to his own Vedantic interpretation of the non-dual absolute. "Is this God of the Hebrew Bible the same as Shiva?" Campbell asked Buber during a question-and-answer period. Buber replied, as I anticipated, by saying that no one could get to the heart of other religions from the outside. Buber believed, as he told Campbell, rejecting the perennial philosophy approach to the study of religion, that each religion was based on a unique revelation that did *not* make them one. Some years later, I read in one of Campbell's books his account of this interchange and was shocked by the distortions that he consciously or unconsciously introduced into his story, the effect of which was to make Buber look bad and himself good! In the summer of 1998, more than forty years after this interchange, the *Journal of the American Association of Religion* published my essay "Why Joseph Campbell's Psychologizing of Myth Precludes the Holocaust as Touchstone of Reality," in which I also took a stand against Campbell's universalizing of religion. When I told Buber that Joseph Campbell had early on edited and translated a book of Heinrich Zimmer's, who was also into universalizing myths, Buber exclaimed, "I could tell that that is where Campbell was coming from." Buber had known Zimmer for many years.

After Martin and Paula had left America, Buber wrote me from Zurich on May 28, 1957, after a long and fruitful journey: "We have not been very well this month, but now it is somewhat better. Sunday we are going to the South of Tyrol, to take some weeks of real rest." While Buber's second trip to America was not as demanding as the first since he refused most lecture invitations, including one from the University of Chicago, it still left him exhausted. Our correspondence continued, of course, as it had in the years past.

9

Postscript to *I and Thou*

Letters Following Buber's Second Visit

In the late summer of 1957, Buber was planning a trip to Munich for a June 1958 conference. Buber had agreed to share a platform with Martin Heidegger, "who," Buber wrote to me, "is more to my taste than his writings." He had had what he called a "very interesting" meeting with Heidegger shortly after leaving America. Heidegger was the leading German existentialist philosopher who had joined the Nazis in their early years and spoke of Hitler as "lord of the hour," as Buber pointed out in "Religion and Modern Thinking" (in *Eclipse of God*). When I asked Buber how he could meet with a former Nazi, he replied, "I have already said what I have to say against him in my essay." Buber's topic on the platform with Heidegger in Munich was to be *"Die Wirklichkeit der Sprache"* ("The Reality of Speech"), but the conference was cancelled due to the death of Paula Buber on the way home from America in the late spring of 1958.

Buber had also, shortly after his second departure from America, begun to draft a preface to *I and Thou* that, it turned out, was published as a postscript. At Buber's request, I prepared a list of questions for him about *I and Thou* that he used as the basis for his postscript. A good many of my questions, however, would remain unanswered until the publication of the Buber volume of the Library of Living Philosophers and *Review of Metaphysics* because the questions required very specific answers.

Though Buber was dealing with an exhausting schedule of writing, lecturing, and traveling, when I failed to write for a couple of months he was kind enough to note, "I think you are overworked, which is not a good thing at all." It was not a good thing, but keeping up with Buber, along with my teaching schedule, was, I confess, not an easy thing to do.

At around this time, a sculptor named Erna Weill, who belonged to a monthly Buber discussion group I hosted that grew out of a course that I gave at the New School for Social Research in New York City, did a sculpture of Buber's head. "The 'Buber,'" Martin told me, "is too 'monumental' for me." Once, when the group was planning to discuss the Hasidic tales, we invited the well-known author (and my Harvard classmate) Norman Mailer to join our discussion. Mailer, who had written an article titled "On Reading Buber's Hasidic Tales during Nights on the Electric Wire of Marijuana," replied that he would decline this invitation since being with people who actually knew something about the subject would interfere with his creativity. The group wanted to send Buber a tape recorder, but he begged them not to, saying it would cost him twice as much in duties as the recorder was worth.

In the years 1957 and 1958, much of our correspondence involved a new edition of *I and Thou*, for which Buber wrote his postscript, originally intended as a new introduction. For Buber scholarship, and for the philosophy of Martin Buber in general, a number of decisions were made for the new edition that are at least philosophically important. Perhaps most importantly, Smith followed my objection—in *The Life and Dialogue*—to using the word "reversal" for *Umkehr* instead of the more precise and theologically interesting "turning" to describe the direction one takes in opening up to dialogue. Avoiding the Christo-centric term "salvation" for the German *Erloesung*, Smith used the term "redemption" instead, a more accurate term that better expresses the Judaic roots of Buber's thought.

Buber, as I have noted above, added a Postscript, originally intended as an introduction, to the new edition of *I and Thou*. Of the series of questions that I wrote to Buber at his request about his book in order to help him plan the Postscript, the one that concerned me the most personally was how the I-Thou relationship between person and person relates to the I-Thou between the human being and God. Since this remains a difficult problem for Buber's readers to grasp, I quote his 1957 reply in full. Buber wrote:

> One must take care not to understand this conversation with God . . . as something happening solely alongside or above the everyday. God's speech to men penetrates what happens in the world around us, biographical and historical, and makes it for you and me into instruction, message, demand. Happening upon happening, situation upon situation are enabled and empowered by the personal speech of God to demand of the human person that he take his stand and make his decision. Often enough we think there is nothing to hear, but long before we have ourselves put wax in our ears. The evidence of mutuality between God and man cannot be proved, just as God's existence cannot be proved. Yet he who dares to speak of it, bears witness and calls to witness him to whom he speaks—whether that witness is now or in the future.

If man was guilty of sometimes putting wax in his ears, thus unable to hear the voice of God, God himself, as the Hebrew Bible attests, "at times hides his face." "What is meant thereby," Buber wrote to me, "is that God answers the withdrawal of man" and not that man cannot hear God because God first fell silent. "I have interpreted the 'silence' of God in just this sense in an earlier section of this book [*I and Thou*]," Buber explained, but in the afterword, he stated, "I am concerned only with the human side, with the great going astray of the human being, to recognize which in its essence and its questionableness is the true task of this book." To read *I and Thou* as a book about the going astray of humankind from God is to understand Buber's "true task" in writing it. At the same time, the book does not despair of this going astray, this turning away. As I wrote in February 1958 in a letter to Buber on the occasion of his eightieth birthday, "you have been for me an image of man as no one else in our time—a life that is courageous and honest, yet real and human and meaningful. You have shown me again and again an alternative to despair."

In 1958 I conducted a series of programs on WBAI radio in New York (now a Pacifica radio station) in honor of Buber's eightieth birthday. Soon after, a young woman (certainly young relative to Buber's years) sent me a letter attesting to the influence of Buber on both herself and a woman she was helping. "I am a voluntary worker for the Guild for the Blind," the letter began:

> I read *I and Thou* to a woman who is totally blind. Let me correct this statement. I did not read "to" her, I read "with" her—at the rate of an hour a week. The spirit within the covers of the book became virtually illuminated. Her response developed to the point where deep problems and tense family relationships were brought to the surface, struggled with, and eventually brought to a state of reconciliation. I should say that the conditions necessary to a therapeutic relationship were naturally fulfilled, and what followed was a natural therapeutic situation in which she grappled with and resolved her problems. More than a year has passed in which the benefits have appeared to be lasting. I witnessed a self-analysis. I quote my friend—
>
> "You became a voice. It was just Martin Buber and myself."
>
> I discovered that reading Buber in this way reveals the deeper layers—it is a realization of Dialogue. The ideas expressed in this book leap into living reality.

This letter, amid my work, gave me a moment to pause and reflect on why I was drawn to Buber's work in the first place: the great presence of dialogue itself that emerges when one reads it deliberately and turns toward it in the same spirit in which it was written.

In 1958 Fritz Kaufmann, the philosopher who was adviser for our *Philosophy of Martin Buber* volume, and who had just retired from teaching and moved to Switzerland near the resting place of his beloved Thomas Mann, died, an event that saddened us deeply. Two years earlier, Buber had written to Kaufmann that he was strictly against Marvin Fox as the only editor of *The Philosophy of Martin Buber*, explaining that he believed I was "necessary in order to assure the equilibrium. Marvin Fox was an American philosopher and Orthodox rabbi whose article on Buber's ethics for *The Philosophy of Martin Buber* was highly critical of Buber, arguing, among many other things, that Buber was an "individualist." Buber, who had been concerned with community and religious Socialism from his earliest writings, told me, after reading the article, "This is a new thing for my old age." Hearing of Buber's response, Fox asked me if Buber would be willing to talk with him when he was next in Jerusalem. I assured him that Buber would and told Buber about the conversation. Buber, as usual, was completely open to meeting any person, no matter how critical that person was. His twice mentioning Fox's failure to come to see him in his letters to me showed that Buber would really have liked to talk with him. Fritz Kaufmann had written a remarkable book on Mann and had defended Mann's *Joseph in Egypt* series against Buber, who felt that Mann's biblical interpretations were actually unbiblical, and to whom he was also very close. "The death of Fritz Kaufmann has been for me too a great shock," Buber wrote to me. "I felt deeply, once more, the cruel fate of human planning—and the great Nevertheless."

10

Buber's Last Visit to America

In the spring of 1958 Buber came to America for the last time at the invitation of the Institute for Advanced Studies at Princeton University where, by a happy coincidence, his old friend Albert Einstein was also present. This was the shortest of his three visits to America, lasting only two months. Kitty McCaw, a donnee of mine, drove us to pick Buber up at the airport. When Kitty met Buber, she asked him if he would meet with a group of Sarah Lawrence students, to which Buber agreed.

Martin Buber and I worked together many hours in the basement of the home of Malcolm Diamond, a professor of religion at Princeton University who had published a book on Martin Buber as religious existentialist. We worked together both on Buber's "Replies to My Critics" for *The Philosophy of Martin Buber* and his answers to the short questions in the Buber sections of Sydney and Beatrice Rome's *Philosophical Interrogations*.

At Buber's request, I translated both of these rejoinders, and as usual we spoke together of problems in my translations. These were, I believe, the last of my translations of Buber. By then, I had translated most of Buber's *Eclipse of God: Studies in the Relation of Religion and Philosophy*, his *The Knowledge of Man* (for which I wrote an introductory essay that became chapter one), all of Buber's *Legend of the Baal Shem, The Tales of Rabbi Nachman, Pointing the Way: Collected Essays, Hasidism and Modern Man, The Origin and Meaning of Hasidism, Daniel: Dialogues on Realization* (for which I also wrote a long introductory essay), *Meetings: Autobiographical Fragments*, and *Elijah: A Mystery Play*.

Once, as we were working together, Buber asked me, "What did you do to get involved with *the* Buber?" recognizing humorously that he had become a sort of institution in the world. Another time, as he descended the stairs to the basement, he fixed me with a wordless look of inquiry that bore into my very soul—a look that I shall never forget! I did not attempt in any way to answer his silent query, which could not, in any case, be put into words.

One of the high points of Buber's 1958 visit to America was a meeting that the American Friends of Ihud sponsored to commemorate his eightieth birthday on February 8. This was also the tenth anniversary of the death of his colleague and friend Judah Magnes, a leading spirit of Ihud and founder and first chancellor of the Hebrew University of Jerusalem. A number of prominent people spoke on this occasion, in addition to Buber himself, such as the noted American psychologist who came originally from Germany, Erich Fromm, and Roger Baldwin, head of the American Civil Liberties Union. Toward the end of the meeting, I got into an unpleasant altercation in front of quite a few members of the audience with Isidor Hoffman, Jewish Chaplain of Columbia University and the oldest member of our executive council. Isidor insisted that Erich Fromm should speak last rather than Martin Buber, as had been planned. Since the meeting was in honor of Martin Buber and Fromm was a known anti-Zionist, I held my ground and insisted that Buber, and not Fromm, should close the meeting.

After the meeting, I naively told Don Peretz that I was going to resign as chairman of the American Friends of Ihud in order to raise the issue of the extent to which quite a number of the members of our executive committee seemed to be much closer to the notorious anti-Zionist organization the American Council for Judaism than to the Zionism that Ihud in Israel expounded.

Instead of allowing me to raise the issue at the next meeting of the executive committee, Peretz gathered all the other members for a meeting without me and, unbeknownst to me, told them I was going to resign as chairman. He then had himself elected chairman in my place.

At one point Peretz and I were going to edit a collection of essays of noted Israelis who all took the Ihud position. Ihud had advocated a binational state with parity of population between Jews and Arabs as the only way to avoid the war that did, in fact, come. This is what in general was known of Ihud in Israel. Since the establishment of the State of Israel in 1948, Ihud had accepted the state as it was and wanted to go from there. This fact was less known in Israel and still less in America. When Buber was in America, he asked me why I had agreed to work with Ihud in the first place. I told him that while I was no authority on Jewish-Palestinian relations in Israel, I felt that perhaps my sympathy for the cause would enable me to do what needed to be done. "That was a mistake!" Buber exclaimed, leaping up from his chair and touching me on the shoulder. I was struck by the fact that he could not tell me how he felt without touching me physically.

In speaking of the policies of the State of Israel, Buber lamented the fact that many Israelis seemed to want to follow the Nazis in holding that the end justified the means. When the American Jewish press picked this up, claiming that a *majority* of the Jewish people learned from Hitler that power was key to maintaining a society, Buber was astounded. In the notes for his speech, as Buber clarified to me in a letter later in the year, he had actually written, "In the days of Hitler the majority of the Jewish people saw that Hitler killed millions of Jews with impunity, and a certain part [of the Jewish people] made their own the doctrine that history does not go the way of the spirit but the way of power." Buber's detractors had mixed up Buber's claim for what a majority of Jewish people had seen in Germany with his claim for how *a certain part* of them transferred their lessons from Hitler to statecraft.

"On further reflection," Buber wrote to me from Soglio, Switzerland, "I feel myself obliged to write down, for the American Jewish press, a clear and precise explanation of my views of the evolution of the Zionist movement and especially its crisis in the days of Hitler and the consequences of this crisis till to-day." Instructing me to send his article to all the Jewish newspapers in America, "or . . . to one that will give it a large publicity," Buber expressed to me that he was "sorry for the confusion that I have caused concerning the Hitler passage. I do not exactly understand how I did it. My heart cannot recover from it because here, as far as I see, is the first negative sign of old age, and I had hoped to be spared. I like to be old," he added. "I like the strange experiences of old age, I like even the burdens and difficulties, but I hate causing confusion." Writing his clarification for the Jewish-American journal *Haaretz*, Buber wrote, "I oppose now, as I opposed then, with all my force those who believe in the doctrine of 'not by the spirit but by power' and actualize it."

A number of students, mostly my own donnees and members of the philosophy seminar at Sarah Lawrence, went to Princeton with me for Buber's seminars there. We had prepared carefully for the meeting. I suggested that each young woman ask Buber one question and warned them that he would only answer "real questions." Each of my students did indeed have a real question ready. As well as I knew these students, something happened at this meeting that I was entirely unprepared for. Without Buber's explicitly asking them to do so, one after another of these students told the concrete event that lay behind her question. One of these had asked what I initially thought a foolish question: "Can one have an I-Thou relationship with someone who is dying?" After she asked this question, she told us of how she sat by the bedside of her dying mother when she was sixteen years old. This question struck Buber so forcibly that he spoke of it when Eugenia and I went to the boat to see Paula and him off on his return trip to Israel.

One student whom I only got to know really well in the months and years after this meeting told of wandering in a sort of schizophrenic trance. The way Buber responded to her concern struck me because he looked at me as if I should have been able to help this student with her problem. Although I had good and even deep relationships with my donnees, up till then I had thought only of the college psychologist as the person who could help such a student. It would occur to me later that Buber was probably thinking of remarks he made in an essay on Hans Trüb, "Healing through Meeting." This essay became the heart of "dialogical psychotherapy" that is based on our genuine interconnections with others.[1]

11

Interrogations and Responses

Letters Following Buber's Last Visit

On August 2, 1958, shortly after leaving America for the third time, Buber wrote to me from Venice that his "wife has been taken ill here a few days ago (a thrombosis but seemingly not a very grave one)." Since their ship to Haifa was not scheduled to depart until the end of the month, Paula Buber was checked into a hospital on the Lido. Seven days later, on August 10, Buber wrote to tell me:

> My wife died two days ago. Her strong heart resisted first to a new hemorrhaging and then to a pulmonitis [pneumonia] for days and days, till it could not resist anymore. We have buried her (I and my children) in the old cemetery of the Jewish community here on the Lido [near a] hill of old trees. Some days before her death she had uttered suddenly, "The grave of Platon [the German poet] in Syracuse."

Paula was very probably unconsciously aware that her own death was approaching and that she, like Platon, a gifted German writer, would be buried abroad. Martin Buber and his children scheduled a return to Israel on August 15.

Eugenia and I were "terribly sorry that your wife's illness turned out, after all, to be fatal and that you are deprived of your lifetime companion." We were both very touched by the way in which Buber wrote while at the same time deeply grieved by what he wrote. "Your wife knew, I am certain," I told Buber, "a fullness and wholeness of life such as is given very few women to know. I can imagine how much you must miss her and how hard it is for you to go on without her. I hope that our love and that of many, many friends the world over will be of help to you now." After he got back to Israel Buber wrote me, "Working now is like walking against the wind." He felt his life utterly disrupted and gave up all plans for lectures, including the one in Munich he was to share with Martin Heidegger.

Buber, meanwhile, was seeking new contributors to the Library of Living Philosophers volume, two of which he wrote to me about, neither of which ever materialized. He wrote in September 1953 that he had spoken to the Israeli novelist S. Y. Agnon, who Buber described as "our greatest novelist," about adding his "great knowledge of Hasidism" to the book. Agnon offered to revise a "rather short" article he had written that had "the character of an authoritative statement." Buber also considered contacting Joseph Weiss from Leeds and Manchester, "a former disciple of Scholem, who has a deep knowledge of Hasidism and is an independent thinker." "It is true he writes slowly," Buber added, "so you could at best get only a short article from him. But I think Agnon's and his would go very well together as the statement of a poet and that of a scholar." No article by either Agnon or Joseph Weiss appeared in the volume. Buber, at the time, was writing his "Responses" to the contributors to the volume, which he intended to publish in a German journal such as *Merkur*.

Buber was also seeking a publisher for a Hebrew translation of *The Life of Dialogue*, and spoke to "the temporary secretary of the Jerusalem Board of the Leo Baeck Foundation" about the book. "If he sees a chance for it, I will speak to the president of the Board." He added, "I would like very much to have you and dear Eugenia here," which would finally happen in 1960, on the eve of Buber's death. Continuing with his writing, Buber began laying plans "to write down the two anthropology chapters" on the topic of "The Unconscious." Sadly, these were never written. All we have today on this topic is what Buber said on the subject at the seminars of the Washington School of Psychiatry.[1] In the course of the winter and spring of 1958 and 1959, Buber decided, he "must go on with the re-translation of the rest of the last Bible volume from Hebrew to German." In particular, "Job must be re-translated." Elucidating a question I had asked him, he let me know that in his book *Hasidism and Modern Man*, he intended to be speaking of three related spheres: "1) of 'the innermost unity of both spheres,' the religious and the ethical, 2) of 'the unity of God's world,' and 3) of man's helping (according to the mystical tradition accepted by Hasidism) 'to effect the unity of the divine forces and forms.'"

Work, Buber wrote to me in late September, "is the only earthly help in my present situation," and in October he wrote that "I am obliged now to bring more order in my whole work, and I will be grateful to you if you will assist me in this." I was planning to help bring to pass an autobiography of Buber, a task that he considered "rather a heavy one as I do not have that kind of memory (the continuity memory) sufficiently." His plan was "to limit myself to recording the fine points most important for the development of my thought." "As to the Autobiography," he had already told me, "I think I shall not be able to give a continuous narration, but only a characterization of the main points." We had begun working together on an autobiographical section for the Library of Living Philosophers, and he emphasized that "I want to tell only of those events or situations that have influenced my thought." He planned to complete the autobiography, "although my state of health is yet of a great liability." A year later, Buber was laying plans to prepublish these "Autobiographical Fragments" in various journals.

At about this time—in September 1958—Buber was informed by the rector of the *Université de Paris* that they wanted to confer upon him an honorary doctorate of the *Faculté des ettres.* This caused him, in a letter to me, to reflect upon the differences between German and French academic life. What "philosophical anthropology means," he told me, "is better understood in German. What an image of man means is better understood in French. But," he added, "I do not know Paris (I mean its academic life) well enough." The main difference between Germany and France "seems to me to be this: in Paris, you can find everything, although not always easily, but in a German university town you can only find this or that."

What Buber called "the Paris meeting" at which he received this doctorate he felt later was too "official," but Florence, he thought, "was very good." By "Florence," Buber meant an occasion on which the mayor of Florence invited representatives from Israel and the other Middle Eastern countries to talk—something that could not have taken place in Israel or any of the Middle Eastern countries themselves. This event, for Buber, was the highlight of the Paris meeting. "When after the lecture of a very gifted Egyptian I invited him to sit with me at the presidential table and to talk the problems over before all," Buber wrote to me after the meeting, "we did it thoroughly and directly. It was," he thought, "rather a symbolical moment."

Over the course of 1959, we were working on a series of questions-and-answers to and from Buber that would be published in *Philosophical Interrogations,* a collection of interviews with influential living philosophers, including Paul Tillich. Originally, these interviews were to be published in the *Review of Metaphysics* across four issues, after which Buber intended to publish them in *Interrogations.* Buber, citing his ill health and age, decided to try to publish his section of *Philosophical Interrogations* early. I was translating the text of the "interrogations," selected all the contributors to the Buber section, and organized and edited their questions. I divided the Buber section, which occupies the first 117 pages of

Philosophical Interrogations, into questions concerning The Philosophy of Dialogue, Theory of Knowledge, Education, Social Philosophy, Philosophy of Religion, The Bible and Biblical Judaism, and Evil. In my introduction to these *Interrogations*, I pointed out that they were really more dialogical than either his essays or his replies to questioners in *The Philosophy of Martin Buber* since, in the *Interrogations*, both the questions and the replies were short and direct.

Of the answers Buber gave to my questions for this volume, one stood out as of particular importance, especially since I realized from Buber's reply that I had been, without knowing it, trying to get him to adumbrate a metaphysics, which he of course refused to do:[2]

Maurice S. Friedman: Does the relation to the Eternal Thou include not only the temporal I-Thou relation, but the I-It relation too?

Explanation: In *I and Thou* you speak of the meeting with the temporal Thou as at the same time a meeting with the Eternal Thou: "In each process of becoming that is present to us, . . . in each Thou we address the eternal Thou, "the Thou in which the parallel lines of relations meet." But you also speak of the relation to the Eternal Thou as summons and sending and of the primal twofold movement of "estrangement from" and "turning toward" the primal Source.

Every real relation in the world is consummated in the interchange of actual and potential being, but in pure relation—in the relation of man to God—potential is still actual being. . . . By virtue of this great privilege of pure relation there exists the unbroken world of Thou which binds up the isolated moments of relation in a life of world solidarity.

Does this mean that we relate to the actual and present Eternal Thou even when the temporal Thou has again become only past and potential, that is, when Thou has again become? Is it not through a continuing relation with the Eternal Thou that we are able ever again to find the Thou, either with the person who was Thou for us but is now It, or with some other whom we have never before met as Thou? If we know the unique value of another only in the I-Thou relationship, is it not the potentiality of his being, or again being a Thou for us, that ultimately prevents our treating the man whom we do not know as Thou purely as a dispensable It? And does not his "personal Thou" rest not only in the "actual Thou" of remembered I-Thou relationships, but on the "actual Thou" of Present Reality—the relation to the Eternal Thou "in which potential is still actual being"? Is it not our trust in the Eternal Thou that gives actuality and continuity to our discontinuous and often merely potential relations to the human Thou?

Buber replied:

I perceive in this question, from words of mine which have been quoted here, that I have already come close to the limit of what is accessible to our experience. I hesitate to go a step further with words the full responsibility for which I cannot bear. In our experience, our relation to God does not include our I-It relation. What is the case beyond our experience, thus, so to speak, from the side of God, no longer belongs to what can be discussed. Perhaps I have here and there, swayed by the duty of the heart that bids me point out what I have to point out, already said too much.

My question to Buber contained the germ of a position that I took in the concluding chapter on "The Image of Man and Moral Philosophy" in my 1967 book *To Deny Our Nothingness: Contemporary Images of Man*. "It is, of course," I wrote there,

essential for an ethic of personal relation that there be a continuity of being responsible for a Thou as well as responding to him . . . otherwise continuing, committed relationships, such as friendship, love, and marriage, would be unthinkable, not to mention the helping relationships of teacher and student, therapist and patient, pastor and congregant. Spontaneity does not mean gratuitous, arbitrary action; for response with the whole being involves all that one has been, including one's past relationships with this person and others and one's image of man.

It is only in a direct, mutual relationship that I grasp concretely the unique value of the other, experience his side of the relationship, and know what can help him. Yet I do not cease to deal lovingly with him or at least respectfully when he is no longer Thou for me in any but a formal or potential sense. I carry from one moment of meeting to the other the form of relationship. I carry the other with me, as it were, as one to whom I am responsible, one to whom I am ready to respond when I meet him again. But when I meet him again, he will not be the same as he was before, and very often I must meet someone with whom I have had no previous real relationship. It is the image of man and not any universal precept that enables me to say, "Nothing human is alien to me." The image of man enters into and forms that attitude that enables me to meet any man whatever as a human being with real human dignity, someone I stand open to know, respect, and perhaps even to love. Thus the image of man plays an essential role in linking one moment of real dialogue with another. It is, often, the very form in which dialogue remains potential, awaiting actualization.[3]

To this part of my question Buber did not respond.

One of Buber's replies in the *Philosophical Interrogations* that struck me since I am both philosopher and teacher was what Buber wrote to Robert Maynard Hutchins concerning Socrates:

I know of few men in history to whom I stand in such a relation of both trust and veneration as Socrates. But when it is a matter of using "Socratic questions" as an educational method, I am against it. I agree, indeed—with some qualifications—to

the statement of Confucius that in order to clarify human realities one must clarify concepts and names, but I am of the opinion that such clarification should be united with a criticism of
the function of concepts and names. Confucius overvalued the
significance for the life of man of designations in comparison
with proper names; Socrates overvalued the significance of
abstract general concepts in comparison with concrete individual experience. General concepts are the most important stays
and supports, but Socrates treated them as if they were more
important than bones—that they are not. Stronger, however,
than this basic objection is my criticism of pedagogical appli-
cation of the Socratic method. Socrates conducts his dialogue
by posing questions and proving the answers that he received
untenable. These are not real questions; they are moves in a
sublime dialectical game that has a goal, the goal of revealing
a not-knowing. But when the teacher whom I mean (apart from
the questions he must ask in examinations) enters into a dialogue with his pupil and in this connection directs a question
to him, he asks, as the simple man who is not inclined to dialectic asks because he wishes to know something: that, namely,
which this young person before him, and precisely he, knows
to report on the subject under discussion: a small individual
experience, a nuance of experience that is perhaps barely conceptually comprehensible, nothing further, and that is enough.
The teacher will awaken in the pupil the need to communicate
of himself and the capacity thereto, and thereby bring him to
greater clarity of existence. But he also learns himself, through
teaching thus; he learns to know concretely the becoming of the
human creature that takes place in experiences; he learns what
no man ever learns completely, the particular, the individual,
the unique. No, certainly no full partnership, but nevertheless a
kind of reciprocity, still a real dialogue.[4]

One short reply of Buber's that I particularly cherish and
often think of came in connection with his interrogation by the

great American philosopher William Ernest Hocking. Hocking asserted that if there is an absolute good, then there must also be an absolute evil. Buber replied, "We encounter every day relative stupidity. Does that mean that there is an absolute stupidity?"[5]

By February 1959, Buber was very ill. "My illness has reached, it seems, its crisis while I was translating the Hebrew Bible over the last two weeks," he wrote to me. "Since the day before yesterday, I have the impression that I am returning to normal life, but very slowly." Still recovering from the Asiatic flu, Buber was concerned that I would be unable to translate the *Autobiography* as soon as I received it in the German. If I was sure this could happen, Buber planned to "put the Bible aside and do my best to finish the Autobiography." At the time, Buber was working on the final unfinished chapters of his translation of the Hebrew Bible into German. I, meanwhile, was planning one book on the image of God and one on the image of man. "I see no objection to your writing a book on 'the image of God,' Buber wrote to me that April, "as long as you keep the two book plans distinct in your thought from one another." "This and that," Buber believed, should never be "intertwined." Ultimately, I wrote the latter—*To Deny Our Nothingness: Contemporary Images of Man* (1967)—but not the former.

That April, a German broadcasting station asked Buber if he would be ready, when in Germany, to read some chapters from the *Autobiography*. Ediciones Iman of Buenos Aires had published some translations of Buber's books into Spanish, and an Ediciones's editor, also in April, expressed interest to Buber in seeing *Martin Buber: The Life of Dialogue* translated, which he believed "would be of great value for a better understanding of your works which I admire so much." So far as I know, no Spanish translation of this book of mine was ever published. Thirty years later, my book *Encounter on the Narrow Ridge: A Life of Martin Buber* was published in Buenos Aires in two separate Spanish-language editions. That April, I also enclosed to Buber my letter of resignation as chairman of the American Friends of Ihud. "It is a mixture of personal conflict and divergence in principle," I wrote in this letter. I regretted "that it had to happen in this way with mistrust all the way round." In exasperation, I confessed that "I don't know the answer to it."

Buber thought the title of my book *Encounter on the Narrow Ridge*, which I had begun under the shorter title *The Narrow Ridge*, a suitable one. Originally, I was going to call it *Martin Buber: The Life of Dialogue on the Narrow Ridge*. A quarter-century after Buber's death, I resurrected this working title and finished the book as *Encounter on the Narrow Ridge: A Life of Martin Buber*. Whereas none of Buber's attempts to get *The Life of Dialogue* published in translation ever succeeded, *Encounter on the Narrow Ridge* has to date been published in Spanish, German, and Japanese, perhaps a signal of growing interest in Buber.

Buber was becoming increasingly tired and several of the works he started in these latter years were never completed. For instance, he was planning an essay—to be published as a chapter in the Library of Living Philosophers volume—on Wilhelm Dilthey and Georg Simmel. "I cannot write it," he said, "because my brain in this physical state does not incline to abstraction, and this chapter is a somewhat abstract one." By December 1959, Buber's autobiographical chapter was yet unwritten. "I have been utterly unable (I mean my soul has been)," he told me, "to write another autobiographical chapter. It is a kind of disinterestedness in my past that has overcome me." Buber's remarkable essay on Krakauer's portrayals of the landscape of Jerusalem in the Munich journal *Merkur*, however, was published that year.

At the time, I was working at Pendle Hill, a Quaker Study Center in Wallingford, Pennsylvania, where Eugenia and I had spent many years teaching, advising, and, in my case, lecturing. Douglas Steere, the chairman of the board at Pendle Hill, wanted

Pendle Hill to have a new program centered around a focal issue—"the image of man"—and they asked me to be the director of studies to get the program going. This was very tempting to me, particularly since the whole program would center around one of my central themes. The program would focus on the image of man in, first, biblical terms, then in terms of the great religions, and finally in terms of contemporary issues. My colleague Helen Lynd questioned whether it would be wise for me to apply for a second year's leave from Sarah Lawrence with the college in transition. A new president and a new dean were to begin their terms the next year. On reflection, I was convinced that I must remain at Sarah Lawrence.

Eugenia and I, meanwhile, began laying more plans for our visit to Jerusalem. "An agency," Buber informed me at the end of 1959, "has offered to my granddaughter an apartment of 3 rooms for 180 Israeli pounds monthly. If you want it, I advise to cable." Buber's granddaughter Barbara, who lived with Buber along with her husband in Talbiyeh after the death of Paula, went to considerable effort to find an apartment for Eugenia and I for our planned four-month stay.

12

Our Stay in Jerusalem
and Buber's Last Years

In January 1960, a long-standing dream of Eugenia's and mine was fulfilled when we went for four months to stay in Jerusalem. Buber's granddaughter Barbara (the sister of Judith, whom I had met in Michigan) found an apartment for us. She was generally helpful in other ways, such as taking us to Abu Tor to show us the house in the Arab section of Jerusalem where the Bubers had formerly lived. She lived with her husband in a house in Talbiyeh where Martin and Paula had lived since the inception of the State of Israel.

Twice a week during our stay we spent a long evening with Martin Buber in his house. There, on several occasions, Buber and Eugenia read together from the koine Greek of the New Testament, Greek being Buber's favorite language after Hebrew.

We also spent some time with a Sarah Lawrence student's uncle who was a lawyer but also ambassador to Israel from two small South American countries. He told us of his love of Greek and his translation of Plato into Hebrew. Since he was so much into Greek I told him that I had translated fairly recently Buber's essay "What Is Common to All," which takes off from some sayings of the great pre-Socratic philosopher Heraclitus. "Buber does not know enough Greek to write about Heraclitus," he asserted. I did not tell him that Greek was Buber's second-favorite language, which he had studied and read since he was small. But, the Sarah Lawrence student's uncle added, "It was all right for Nietzsche, who also did not really know Greek, since Nietzsche was a philosopher." "Is then Buber not a philosopher?" I asked him. "Why, he has lived around the corner from me for fourteen years!" he exclaimed.

At about midnight on our visits, Buber would still be going strong while Eugenia and I would begin fading on the vine. Buber and I got a lot of work done together during this period, and I was able to ask him most of the questions that had arisen for me from his writings. At one point, he took me into his study and showed me, in the Hebrew, the section of the Book of Job that he had interpreted for the American philosopher Walter Kaufmann at the latter's request. A few years later, I published an article in response titled "Walter Kaufmann's Mismeeting with Buber."[1]

During our visit, Buber renewed his pressure on me to get the Buber volume of the Library of Living Philosophers as well as his section of the *Philosophical Interrogations* published. I could not do anything about the former since the Buber volume had to wait till after a volume on Carnap was published. ("If I had a following like Carnap, I should want my volume published soon too!" Buber exclaimed.) In 1964, however, a year before Buber's death, I succeeded in finding a publisher for the *Interrogations*. Originally, they were to be published as a whole issue of *The Review of Metaphysics*. Since this was no longer the plan, I approached my old friend Arthur Cohen, now an editor at Holt, Rinehart & Winston, and he agreed to bring out the *Philosophical Interrogations* as a book.

But about the *Living Philosophers* volume I could do nothing. Kohlhammer Verlag brought out the German edition of the Buber volume in 1965. But the English edition did not appear in America and Great Britain until 1966, a year after Buber's death. I can very well understand how Buber felt about this volume not getting published in English in his lifetime, particularly given the many friends of his who wanted to see his "Replies to My Critics" in print. I also understand how he felt about me, a young man who could not, as he said repeatedly, understand an old one. He felt this way partly because he did not believe I had an adequate understanding of the exigencies of time, which was particularly poignant for him in the light of his sentence in "Guilt and Guilt Feelings": "Time is like a torrent leading us to the starkest of all human perspectives—one's individual death." I do not think Buber was afraid of death, but I do think he was obsessed by it as the final abandonment that would complete what he felt when his mother left him in the fourth year of his life. While Buber was in Switzerland one summer, a nun said to him that he ought not feel as he did about death. But he did.

None of this changed the fact that I was helpless to do anything about getting out the Buber volume of *Living Philosophers* during his lifetime. Eugenia felt, and I agreed, that Buber was unfair to me on this subject. At one point, when we were at his house in the evening, I said to him that I could almost wish that I had not taken these projects on. The pressure he put on me led me to state that I felt that this remarkable and usually gentle and perceptive man was "the old man of the mountain" riding my back!

After I said this, Buber gave me a sharp look and asked me if I were sorry about everything. I knew he was thinking of Hermann (later Menachem) Gerson. Gerson was so much Buber's disciple in Berlin that he grew a beard like him and imitated him in every way, particularly in his thought. Gerson had not wanted Buber to have too much contact with the *Werklelute*, or working people, who Gerson himself felt some sense of responsibility for. Under his leadership, a group of workers all migrated to Palestine and founded Kibbutz Hazorea, but Gerson's charisma no longer held his followers together, and even his wife left him.

Gerson had become sympathetic with the Mapam, a radical Socialist movement among the kibbutzim in Palestine, and he eventually rejected Buber lock, stock, and barrel, only returning to him a few years before Buber's death. Did I want an estrangement like this?

"Of course not," I replied, knowing that nothing could destroy my sense of indebtedness to Buber and my close resonance with his thought and life. It was, I think, during this time that I came up against Buber most and in so doing encountered a great force that I have never encountered in another human being!

Some time after Buber's death, his great friend Grete Schaeder, who had put together with Buber his *Nachlese*, or *Gleanings*, said to me that she and I had known Buber when he was relatively more whole but that when he was younger she believed he was more unbalanced. Buber himself said to Eugenia and me at one point, "I am no saint. When I was young, I was tempted again and again to push myself and others over into evil."

It was on this trip that Buber told Eugenia and me that Chaim Weizmann, the friend of his youth who had composed with him the first proposal for the Hebrew University in Jerusalem and who was much later the first president of Israel, never forgave him for not writing him when he learned that Weizmann's son had been killed in World War I. We could see that Buber was still troubled by this failure on his part and by Weizmann's reaction to it. "When a person feels something toward another person, should he not speak it out directly?" Buber asked us.

After leaving Israel four months on the other side of our arrival, we next saw Buber in June 1960 when he gave his speech on "The Word That Is Spoken" for his Munich Prize lecture, but I had little real contact with him through 1960. Buber and I continued to correspond, but less and less frequently during the next five years leading up to his death.

In 1960 I published a pamphlet titled "The Covenant of Peace" for Pendle Hill, which Buber called "a good piece of autobiographical information." I was also working on my Kafka chapter, which actually became many chapters or at least a fourth of my book *Problematic Rebel*, originally subtitled *An Image of Modern Man* (published in its most recent edition as *Melville, Dostoevsky, Kafka, Camus*). While we were in Jerusalem, Buber advised me just to focus on Melville and Dostoevsky and skip Kafka ("the man of the hour," as Buber put it). But later he thought so highly of the Kafka section of *Problematic Rebel* that he sent it to Max Brod, Kafka's great friend and posthumous rescuer of the novels that Kafka wanted destroyed along with all the rest of his writings. Eugenia and I met Max Brod in Tel Aviv and had a good talk with him about Kafka's friend Milena Jesenká, among other subjects.

In his review of *Problematic Rebel*, Buber focused especially on my treatment of Kafka. Writing that "*Problematic Rebel* is an important book," he continued:

> It is especially important because its theme is not expounded through concepts but through representative figures of narrative literature of two generations—that of Melville and Dostoevsky and that of Kafka and Camus. The theme is a revolt of man against an emptying of meaning, the existence after the so-called death of God. This emptying is not to be overcome through the illusionary program of a free creation of values, as we know it in Nietzsche and Sartre. One must withstand this meaninglessness, must suffer it to the end, must do battle with it undauntedly until out of the contradiction experienced in conflict and suffering meaning shines forth anew. It is this teaching that the principal figures of these novelists of our era make known to us, although often in an indirect way that demands our cooperation. That Maurice Friedman assigns these figures to two basic types, that of the "Rebel" and that

of the "Exile" and that he brings them into relation with the poetry of antiquity, Prometheus and Job, makes them of still greater value.

During his trip to Munich in 1960, Buber fell seriously ill and recovered very slowly. Not citing his ill health but the great deal of work he had to do in the coming year, Buber told me that he could not make any further plans for traveling abroad. "I have got a warning and must learn to live 'economically,'" he wrote. "This means, of course, not leisure but work. I have got a lot of work for next year." This work included writing a Responsum on Hasidism, which Buber had to interrupt for some days to work on a translation of *Chronicles*, the last book of the *Old Testament*, along with his "Replies to My Critics."

In his replies, Buber eventually offered several responses to my essay "The Bases of Buber's Ethics." One of these seems to me particularly compelling for its treatment of the traditional Buberian theme of redemption:

> Friedman advances as my view: "One's antagonist may, indeed, be the devil or Hitler, but even such a one must be faithfully answered, contended with!" . . . On the one side, I hold no one to be absolutely irredeemable, and if a devil existed, then I would believe that God could redeem him, and even that God would do so. And not that alone, but I could also conceive that God might expect and trust in man for a share in this work of redemption. But as soon as we reflect on it with wholly concrete seriousness, a limit becomes evident that is no longer restricted to the symbolic, like the traditional image of the devil, but bears a wholly empirical character. Here it is no longer for me to speak of God, but solely of myself and this man.
>
> Hitler is not my antagonist in the sense of a partner "whom I can confirm in opposing him," as Friedman says, for he is incapable of really addressing me and incapable of really listening

to me. That I once experienced personally when, if only through the medium of the radio, I heard him speak. I knew that this voice was in the position to annihilate me together with countless of my brothers; but I perceived that despite such might, it was not in the position to set the spoken and heard word into the world. And already less than an hour afterward I sensed in "Satan," the "poor devil" in power, and at the same time I understood my dialogical powerlessness. I had to answer, but not to him who had spoken. As far as a person is a part of a situation, I have to respond, but not just to the person.[2]

I had never heard advanced before that responding to the broader situation created by a man of evil constituted a dialogical response—if one-sided.

It was largely because of Buber's spirit of open dialogue that Dag Hammarskjöld, the Secretary-General of the United Nations, encouraged my nomination of Buber for a Nobel Peace Prize in 1961, which Buber did not receive. Instead, the Swedish Academy awarded the prize to Dag Hammarskjöld himself, who had served as the UN's secretary-general since 1951. Hammarskjöld gave a moving acceptance speech that credited Buber as an important influence on his philosophy of diplomacy. I obtained many distinguished signatures in support of the Buber nomination, including one from T. S. Eliot, who wrote, "I once had a conversation with Dr. Buber, . . . and I got the strong impression that I was in the company of a great man. There are only a very few men of those whom I have met in my lifetime, whose presence has given me that feeling."[3] Ronald Gregor Smith, the original translator into English of I and Thou, had brought Buber and Eliot together in 1951. After Buber's death, an editor of Newsweek got that quotation from me and used "In the Presence of Greatness" as the title of that magazine's article on Buber.

Other signatories to the petition that I sent to the Nobel Committee included Emil Brunner, Albrecht Goes, Victor Gollancz,

Hermann Hesse, Gabriel Marcel, Sir Herbert Read, Ignazio Silone, Wilhelm Szilasi, Max Brod, Arthur A. Cohen, Nahum Norbert Glatzer, Karl Kerenyi, Gershom Scholem, Ernst Simon, Paul Tillich, W. H. Auden, Charles Malik, and Reinhold Niebuhr, all of whom wrote warm and enthusiastic notes to me with their signatures. H. Richard Niebuhr, Reinhold's brother, was invited to sign, but his son wrote me that my letter was on his desk at the time of his death.

Charles Malik, former ambassador to the United Nations from Lebanon and professor at the American University in Beirut, wrote a remarkable assessment of Buber that dealt with the Israeli-Arab conflict as none of the other signatories could have done, from the Arab side of the conflict:

> Buber is one of the important influences for my thought, especially through his *Ich und Du*. I also conceived a high regard for him and the late Dr. Magnes in connection with the Palestine Question. I always felt that he and I would agree on many things, spiritual and political. The type of spirit he represents could still help in bringing about a reconciliation, in God's own time, between Arab and Israeli. If only political passion on both sides would make it possible to "meet," in Buber's sense of the term, in an atmosphere of Christian love and forgiveness! But man is so limited and history is so tragic and the mystery of God is so unfathomable. I trust the Swedish Academy would give this matter their serious consideration, for no living man, in my opinion deserves the Nobel Prize for Literature more worthily than Martin Buber.[4]

Malik added in a personal note to me, "It gives me the greatest personal pleasure to join you and Dr. Niebuhr in this most worthy endeavor. I wish there was something else I could do for this noble soul. Buber is greater than even the fine eulogy you compiled for him in your draft letter."

The draft letter I sent to those we invited to sign the petition read in part:

> We are inviting you and a few other prominent writers and leaders of culture throughout the world to ask you to join in a cause that was dear to the heart of the late Dag Hammarskjold: the choice of Martin Buber for the Nobel Prize in Literature. Hermann Hesse nominated Buber for this award in 1948, and Dag Hammarskjold nominated him twice in the years immediately preceding his death. It is our understanding that Dr. Michael Landman of Berlin has again nominated Martin Buber for a Nobel Prize this coming year.

The nomination letter that we sent to the Nobel Committee of the Swedish Academy read in part:

> Few living writers have made as great a contribution to the literature and culture of our time as has Martin Buber.
>
> Professor Buber has spent a lifetime of work in the re-creation of the legends and teachings of Hasidism, the popular communal mysticism that flourished among the Jews of Eastern Europe in the eighteenth and nineteenth centuries. Through the literary form that he has given it Buber has single-handedly made this heritage an integral part of the culture of Western man. "Martin Buber," writes Hermann Hesse, "has enriched world literature with a genuine treasure as has no other living author." Karl Kerenyi points to Buber's Hasidic chronicle novel *Gog und Magog* (*For the Sake of Heaven*) as justification of his claim that Buber "has won a secure place for himself among the ranks of classical writers in the fullest and deepest sense of the term." The great achievement of this chronicle is its evocation of fighters of the spirit who are without comparison in the whole of epic world literature in the ardor and exclusiveness of their religious powers.

BUBER'S LAST YEARS   ~   151

A second contribution of Martin Buber to the literature and culture of our time is that philosophy of "dialogue" ranging from ethics, social philosophy, and psychotherapy to education, art, and religion that he has set forth in a series of important works written over the last forty years. Buber's *I and Thou*, the classic statement of his I-Thou philosophy, is today universally recognized as one of the masterpieces of the literature and thought of our time. J. H. Oldham, a leader of the ecumenical movement of the Christian church, has written of *I and Thou*, "I question whether any book that has been published in the present century has a message, which if it were understood and heeded, would have such far-reaching consequences for the life of our time."

A third realm in which Buber has made a contribution equally as significant as the literature of Hasidism and of dialogue is his translation and interpretation of the Hebrew Bible. Only this year he has finished the translation of the fourth volume of the Hebrew Bible into German that he began with Franz Rosenzweig in 1926. This translation has preserved the original spoken quality and dialogical meaning of the Bible as no other translation has ever done. In addition, he has written a series of interpretations of the Bible that show prophetic thought to be the source of what today we call existentialism. Reinhold Niebuhr has written [of Buber's biblical interpretations] that they are "a more persuasive form of this philosophy or theology than any system elaborated under Christian auspices."

"Professor Buber," writes the distinguished Old Testament scholar J. Coert Rylaarsdam, "is in a unique way the agent through whom Judaism and Christianity in our day have met and enriched each other."

"Any of these three literatures that Martin Buber has produced," I wrote in closing, "could justify his title to a Nobel Prize in Literature." Buber, in a characteristic spirit of equanimity, wrote, when

I told him of the nomination, "I did not hear anything about the Nobel Prize. As you know, my way is not to ask people at all about such things. I like pleasant surprises, but I do not deal with them in my heart, and their not coming is no disappointment."

Gabriel Marcel, one of the signers, was a distinguished twentieth-century French dialogical existentialist who, partly under the influence of the American philosopher Josiah Royce, developed his *Je-Tu* relationship in his metaphysical journals independently of Buber. The distinguished French philosopher Jean Wahl was visiting professor at the University of Chicago in the late 1940s when I was doing my doctoral work. I discussed with him the remarkable parallels between Marcel's and Buber's philosophy of religion, which he shared with Marcel himself when he returned to Paris. In the first pages of his essay on "Martin Buber and *I and Thou*"—the opening essay in *The Philosophy of Martin Buber*—Marcel seeks the deeper causes of this parallel, while expressing great admiration for Buber's *I and Thou*.

Ernst Simon once told me that Buber probably would have received the Nobel Prize long since if he had not "ruined his life" by going to America so there would have been no political necessity for finding a figure of equal stature in the Arab world. Probably, Buber's association with the State of Israel stymied his receipt of the award.

In February 1962, I had lunch with the editor Arthur Cohen, during which he talked about the possibility of a new company—Holt, Rinehart & Winston—of which he was the religious editor of trade books. He had since written me a letter in which he offered to publish *Daniel: Dialogues of Realization*. Buber consented to publish it on the condition that I write a long introduction explaining its place in his thought, which I did. I believed that Buber was mistaken if he thought that compiling the bibliography for *The Philosophy of Martin Buber* was an easy task. As I wrote him, it was, in fact, a very difficult one. I had by no means relied principally on the Catane, a bibliography that had been prepared in Israel by Mosad Bialik, with Hebrew as well as German and English items. This bibliography accounts for less than a third of the 700 items that I gathered. Buber's doubt about our finishing *The Philosophy*, I believed, was another instance of Buber failing to "imagine the real."

Buber's health, however, continued to suffer, which might explain his pessimism in matters of writing and publishing— not to mention translating—in his later years. On June 12, 1963, Buber wrote that his doctors wanted him to return (after a two-day sojourn in Amsterdam to receive the Erasmus Prize) to the same sanatorium he had retired to the previous year: Sonnmatt, near Lucerne, Switzerland. He planned to stay there from July 8 "till the first September days." He thanked me for my photos of David, our nearly two-year-old adopted son, and sent his love to Eugenia.

In early October, I wrote to Buber that Eugenia and I brought home a daughter, a three-month-old baby whom we named Dvora Lisa. We decided to wait until David was two years old to adopt a second child. As it turned out, Dvora Lisa was born exactly on David's second birthday! We were happy and excited, and so was David, who immediately assumed a proprietary role. "Despite all our anticipation with names," I told Buber, it was "a strange experience of otherness." Dvora has remarkably big round blue eyes that communicate an almost preternatural awareness "so that one feels more looked at than looking." Eugenia had no anxiety about this child, as she had with David, but the work was doubled and our quarters were somewhat cramped for two children.

We were all deeply shocked and grieved by the assassination of President Kennedy and the events that followed. "We have seen no collective pall like it since the end of the Second World War," I told Buber. My first, apocalyptic thoughts were of civil war or of a situation such as that of the Nazis in Germany in 1933, but

I assumed that neither of these would happen. Still the anxiety in the air was very real.

Early in 1964, in February, in fact, I contacted Buber about a Pembroke student who came up to me after a lecture I had given at Brown University and told me that her mother, Marian Spector of Saint Louis, had been corresponding with Buber and had seen him in Israel. She asked me when his cataract operation was to be. I was surprised that she knew about it while I did not. Eugenia and I were anxious to know this, too.

A young cousin of mine, Eddie Goldman, was with the American Student Program in Israel in 1964. He was a brilliant student, a graduate of Harvard, who had spent much time with Tillich. He was studying at Hebrew Union College to become a rabbi. He was a very serious young man and very much wanted to meet Buber. I hoped that if Buber's health and time permitted, he would let Goldman come see him. Eddie Goldman went on to become a member of the faculty of Hebrew Union College and, after that, a dean. Another man I recommended to Buber was an English instructor at Brown University, Alvin Rosenfeld, who had an Eastern European Jewish background, had written a master's thesis on Whitman and Buber, and was much tormented about Judaism, Hasidism, dialogue, and his own way forward. After becoming an expert in the poetry of Paul Celan and going through agonies with a Catholic fiancée, Alvin Rosenfeld went on to become a distinguished professor of English at Indiana University, adviser to the Jewish student program there, and, along with other impressive publications, co-editor of a book on Elie Wiesel to which he contributed an important essay.

Also in 1964, the Jewish Labor Committee—an antireligious Socialist group—was doing a series of six lectures on Buber by various people, most of whom I suggested. I opened this series with a talk titled "Martin Buber as Socialist." My book *The Worlds of Existentialism: A Critical Reader* was also in production, and it turned out to be a monumental task, of which, I vowed, "I shall never do the like again." *The Worlds of Existentialism* was the first really critical, comprehensive reader of existentialism with a long introduction, short introductions to each section, and a long conclusion, all of which I wrote. It totaled 700 pages instead of the projected 500, and as a result it was published as a Vintage paperback instead of a Modern Library edition. One highbrow book club committed themselves to it on the basis of the table of contents alone. Around this time, I translated Buber's "Mystery Play" *Elijah* and sent it to him as a surprise. Later, we had a reading of it at Pendle Hill in which I was Elijah and Eugenia the voice of God. It was produced at Manhattanville College of the Sacred Heart while I was teaching there in the 1966–1967 academic year.

When my father died in February 1965, Buber sent me a kind letter, after which I heard little from him before his death. Dan Wilson, the director of Pendle Hill, came to see me in February to offer his condolences. When Buber died in June, Dan was a great comfort as well. I told Buber that Dan taught *I and Thou* at Pendle Hill, and this particular piece of information from outside Buber's immediate world pleased Buber immensely. When Shulamit Katz-Nelson called with Hugo Bergman and Bergman's wife to visit Buber on his deathbed the same year, Buber told him, "That is not life, Shulamit." Life is what he felt terribly cut off from at that time. "I do not mind being dead," Buber said, "but I mind dying."

In 1951, I had translated "Buecher und Menschen" for Eugenia on her birthday. This beautiful little essay of Buber's ended with the touching statement, "I want to die with a human hand in my own." Sadly, for Buber, this wish was not fulfilled. Before his death, he was abandoned by many of his close friends who either lived too far away or did not want to go see Buber in his shrunken last state. For those who were there, Buber may only have been aware of them dimly through a coma. Although I was hit hard by the news of Buber's death, I did not cry in response to it until 1966 when I was doing research in the Buber Archives of the Jewish National and University Library in Jerusalem for what became my three-volume *Martin Buber's Life and Work*. I saw a display at the Jewish National and University Library of photographs of Buber and his family and friends, including pictures of his grandparents, his mother, his early friends, Paula as a young woman, and others, among whom Buber was standing, holding a sword.

Epilogue

Memorial Address

MARTIN BUBER

MAURICE FRIEDMAN

"What do you think of Martin Buber?" a student of mine once asked Paul Tillich in my presence, obviously expecting some critical intellectual reply.[1] "What do I think of him?" Tillich exclaimed. "I love him." To my student the name "Martin Buber" stood for a collection of books. For Paul Tillich it evoked the presence of a man. For us, too, who come together tonight, the name "Martin Buber" evokes a presence, and our witness to him is a response to this presence. Though one of the truly great writers of this century, Martin Buber confessed that he preferred humans to even the most delightful of books.

> The many bad experiences with [people] have nourished the meadow of my life as the noblest book could not do, and the good experiences have made the earth into a garden for me. On the other hand, no book does more than remove me into a paradise of great spirits where my innermost heart never forgets I cannot dwell long, nor even wish that I could do so. For (I must say this straight out in order to be understood) my innermost heart loves the world more than it loves the spirit. . . . Aye, these tousle-heads and good-for-nothings, how much I love them!

157

I revere books—those that I really read—too much to be able
to love them. But in the most vulnerable of living [persons] I
always find more to love than to revere: I find in [them] something of this world, that is simply there as the spirit never can
be there. . . . I knew nothing of books when I came forth from
the womb of my mother, and I shall die without books, with
another human hand in my own.[2]

The death of Martin Buber has brought home to us the fact
that he was one of the great figures not only of a people but of
humankind, not only for this age but for the ages to come. Our
grief that he is no longer with us must be tempered with gratitude for the "fullness of days" that was allotted to him and with
awe before his ability to "begin anew, to be old in a young way."
Although Buber was famous as a writer from his youth, it was
chiefly in the latter half of his long life that he unfolded that
remarkable productivity in scholarship, original thought, and
literary creativity that makes his contribution to our culture so
astonishingly rich. The man who told me that his books were
merely "snakeskins," which he wrote only as he needed to shed
them, left behind him a heritage of books of a quality, quantity,
and variety such as few authors of our time can claim—biblical
and Hasidic translations and interpretations, philosophy, and
philosophy of religion; essays on art, education, drama, poetry,
psychiatry, social problems, ethics, international relations and
peace, Zionism and Jewish-Arab relations; legends, tales, poems,
even a novel and a play.

In Martin Buber, person and thinker were inseparably con-
joined. He was a philosopher of dialogue only because in the first
instance he lived "the life of dialogue." Many have witnessed that
the most astonishing thing about Buber was the fact that his person did not give the lie to his works. This does not mean that

Buber was a man who lived his ideals. He was not an idealist, but "a realist of the spirit." He was the most insistently and even disconcertingly concrete man I have ever known. The unity of Buber's life and thought was the unity of his person: his words and his actions were equally an expression of his courage, his responsibility, his openness, his readiness to meet the person or situation before him. "Do not withhold yourself," Buber advised, and he practiced his own advice. Yet he knew how to say "No" as well as to say "Yes." He practiced as long as he lived "decision before the Face," and he overcame in his own person that source of conflict between man and man to which he points in *The Way of Man*—the fact that we do not say what we mean and we do not do what we say.

Martin Buber embodied what he himself saw as the essence of all lived religion: presentness. Charismatic force he certainly had, with his penetrating yet kindly eyes. But what was truly remarkable about him was the fact that he was really *present*, as most of us are not, and that *his* presentness encouraged and demanded *ours*. Buber told me of his meeting with Eliot five days after it took place. "Don't you find that your opinions and those of T. S. Eliot differ in important respects?" I asked Buber, thinking of a course I was just then preparing. "When I meet a [person]," Buber said to me, "I am not concerned with his [or her] opinions but with the [person]."

An important part of Buber's presentness was that he did not make of it a spirituality that overpowered the other person but a "listening obedience" that experienced the other person's side of the relationship as well as his own by concretely imagining what the other was thinking, feeling, and willing. I have known many spiritual men, but I have never known a man who really opened himself to the presence of the other in such concreteness as Buber. When I brought six students from Sarah Lawrence to Princeton in 1953 to talk with Buber, I understood better than he the intellectual questions they asked him. I knew these students and their thinking well, and he had just met them. Yet each of these women, without his asking, told him the concrete experience that lay behind the intellectual question, and I witnessed in amazement a new dimension of dialogue that I had not suspected.

My mother visited Martin Buber in Jerusalem in 1950 and brought him my doctoral dissertation on his thought. But Buber's first letter to me was not about my dissertation, which he had not yet read, but about me. It offered to help me; it asked me to write him fully about myself; and it cautioned me against "analyses"— against the substitution of psychological categories for concrete events between people. When I first met Buber in person almost a year and a half later, he told me that he was not interested in me primarily as someone who was writing a book on him but as a person. I knew then and have never doubted since that what he said was true. What gave Buber his imperishable greatness, as the Swiss psychiatrist Hans Trüb said, was that he stepped forth as this single man and talked directly to people. This was true even when Buber lectured to a large audience. In the question period Buber would invariably move until he stood face-to-face with the questioner and then take however long was necessary to reach a real meeting with him or her. In his person as well as in his writings Buber taught us that a real meeting does not mean giving way to the other but responding *and* holding your ground.

In his essay "My Way to Hasidism" Buber contrasts himself with the zaddik, the charismatic figure who was the leader of these popular Jewish mystical communities: "I who am truly no zaddik," he writes, "no one assured in God, rather a man endangered before God, a man wrestling ever anew for God's light, ever anew engulfed in God's abysses."[3] Yet in the almost half century that he lived beyond the essay, he took on ever more powerfully the lines of the "true zaddik" he himself had described:

I mean those who withstand the thousandfold-questioning glance of the individual lives, who give true answer to the trembling mouth of the needy creature who time after time demands from them decision; I mean the zaddikim, the true zaddik. That is the man who hourly measures the depths of responsibility with the sounding lead of his words.[4]

Buber's existence was "continually renewed decision"—from his readiness to meet whoever came to see him to his refusal to deal with unreal questions. (I once heard Buber in this very synagogue ask one man whether he had lain awake all night thinking of the question he was asking.) Buber withstood the "thousand-fold-questioning glance" of countless sorely troubled persons and measured hourly the depths of responsibility with the sounding lead of his presence and his words. In the dialogue between Buber and the American psychologist Carl Rogers that I moderated at the University of Michigan in 1957, Buber said:

I have necessarily to do with the problematic type of [person]. . . . Life has become baseless for [him or her]. [S/he] cannot tread on firm soil, on firm earth. [S/he] is, so to speak, suspended in the air. And what does [s/he] want? . . . a being not only whom [s/he] can trust as a [person] trusts another, but a being that gives [him or her] now the certitude that "there *is* a soil, there *is* an existence. The world is not condemned to deprivation, degeneration, destruction. The world *can* be redeemed. I can be redeemed because there is this trust." And if this is reached, I can help this [person] even in [their] struggle against [him- or herself].[5]

"Trust, trust in the world because this human being exists"—this was Martin Buber's most precious gift, not only to the "problematic person" but to all the persons of our age, to those thousands who knew him only from his writings, his spoken words, his actions.

At a celebration of Buber's eightieth birthday sponsored by the American Friends of the Hebrew University, Martin Buber said of himself: "I am not a prophet, philosopher, or theologian. I am simply a man who has seen something and who goes to the window and points to what he sees." Buber's teaching was, in fact, a pointing far more than it was a defining. The "narrow ridge" that Buber walked was neither philosophy nor religion and certainly not a theology in the usual sense of these terms; nor shall we have more success if we try to understand him through the label "mystic" or "existentialist." Yet Buber has had a revolutionary impact on the religious and theological thought of our time; his stature as a philosopher is being given ever fuller recognition; through his work on Hasidism he has put before the world "a realistic and active mysticism"; and he is the foremost existentialist of dialogue. Many would agree with the statement that the Italian novelist Ignazio Silone made to the Nobel Prize Committee in 1962: "I know of no person at the present moment who is Buber's equal in the profundity of the spirit or in the power and quality of his expression." Charles Malik, the former United Nations ambassador from Lebanon, also wrote the Nobel Prize Committee, "No living man, in my opinion, deserves the Nobel Prize for literature more worthily than Martin Buber." And he added, "The type of spirit Buber represents could still help in bringing about a reconciliation, in God's own time, between Arab and Israeli."

Three of Buber's legacies to the generations to come are well known: his translation and interpretation of the Hebrew Bible; his recreation of Hasidic tales and teachings; and his philosophy of dialogue, or the "I-Thou" relationship. *I and Thou* is recognized as one of the great classics of this century. Hermann Hesse, the Swiss poet and novelist, nominated Buber for a Nobel Prize in Literature in 1948 on the basis of *Tales of the Hasidim* through which Buber "enriched world literature with a genuine treasure as has no other living author." Another of Buber's legacies that is not so well known is his lifelong concern with social problems, which issued into his fruitful distinction between political and social principles and his call for a restructuring of society as a "community of communities." When Dag Hammarskjold announced his intention of translating into Swedish the "Politics, Community, and Peace" section of Buber's *Pointing the Way*, he said of these essays, "I think Buber has made a major contribution, and I should like to make it more broadly known."

Buber's last legacy is his philosophical anthropology, the final stage of which is presented in his shortly to be published book *The Knowledge of Man*. *The Knowledge of Man* is truly the culmination and crown of Buber's philosophy. In it Buber explores the depths of distance and relation, of the interhuman and the social, of neurotic and existential guilt, of psychiatry, art, speech, community. What Buber says of the ontological significance of all philosophical anthropology is especially true of his own: "To the degree that we fathom the relation of a circle of reality to us, we are always referred to its still unfathomed relation to being and meaning." Martin Buber's *Knowledge of Man* refers us with a profundity unequalled in our time to man's still unfathomed relation to being and meaning.

Martin Buber was our comrade. He lived with us, won our trust through real-life relationship, and helped us to walk with him in the way of the creature who *accepts* the creation. Like the great Hasidic rebbe Levi Yitzhak of Berdichev, Buber did not ask to know the secret of God's ways but to know "what this, which is happening at this very moment, means to me, what it demands of me, what you, Lord of the world, are telling me by way of it." "Ah, it is not why I suffer, that I wish to know," cried Levi Yitzhak, "but only whether I suffer for your sake." The innermost core of Buber's teaching and of his existence was just this combination of trust in existence and the acceptance of suffering—the suffering of the righteous person for the sake of redemption and the mystery of

God's nearness in the very pit of suffering. This acceptance of suffering was not incompatible, for Buber, with withstanding God and contending with him. In Buber's play *Elijah*, Elijah cries out, "Ah Lord, I have ever loved you, why do you make it so hard for me to love you?"

In my book *Problematic Rebel: An Image of Modern Man*, I point out that trust and contending mark the "Modern Job"—Kafka and the later Camus—as much as they do the original one. No one has joined trust and contending in his life and thought more clearly than Martin Buber. The question of trust in existence that is at the heart of Job's dialogue with God is equally at the heart of Buber's walking the "narrow ridge" in an age of the "eclipse of God," an age where God's finger seems nowhere to be present in history. "The dialogical leads inevitably to Job's question to God," writes Buber. "My God will not allow to become silent in the mouth of his creature the complaint about the great injustice in the world."

And even when this man knows peace, in the sense that God comes near to him again, this peace is not incompatible with the fight for justice. Nothing for Buber so makes manifest the "eclipse of God"—"the unredeemed concreteness of the human world in all its horror"—as the Nazi's scientific extermination of six million Jews. Buber's response to "the Job of Oswiecim," the "Job of the gas chambers," is again the attitude of the Modern Job:

> We—by that is meant all those who have not got over what happened and will not get over it. How is it with us? Do we stand overcome before the hidden face of God as the tragic hero of the Greeks before faceless fate? No, rather even now we contend, we too, with God, ever with Him, the Lord of Being, Whom we once, we here, chose for our Lord. We do not put up with earthly being, we struggle for its redemption, and struggling we appeal to the help of our Lord, Who is again and still a hiding one. . . .

Though His coming appearance resemble no earlier one, we shall recognize again our cruel and merciful Lord.[6]

In his struggle for Jewish-Arab rapprochement, in his leadership of the German Jews in their "spiritual war" against Hitler, in his reply to Gandhi's criticism of the Jews for settling in Palestine, in his affirmation of the human against the antihuman when he accepted the Peace Prize of the German Book Trade, in his protest against the execution of Eichmann, Buber has shown what it means to be a Modern Job. The Modern Job revolts against an existence emptied of meaning, wrote Buber in a statement on my book *Problematic Rebel*. He does so through withstanding this meaninglessness, suffering it to the end, doing "battle with it undauntedly, until out of the contradiction experienced in conflict and suffering meaning shines forth anew."

In a time in which we are in danger of losing our birthright as human beings, Martin Buber has given us again an image of humans. In a time in which human thought preserves the *idea* of God but destroys the reality of our relationship to him, Buber has pointed us anew to the meeting with the "eternal Thou."

God's speech to [humans] penetrates what happens in the life of each one of us, and all that happens in the world around us, biographical and historical, and makes it for you and me into instruction, message, demand. Happening upon happening, situation upon situation, are enabled and empowered by the personal speech of God to demand of the human person that he take his stand and make his decision. . . .

The existence of mutuality between God and man cannot be proved, just as God's existence cannot be proved. Yet he who dares to speak of it, bears witness, and calls to witness him to whom he speaks—whether that witness is now or in the future.[7]

NOTES

REFERENCES

INDEX

Notes

Foreword

1. Martin Buber, *The Knowledge of Man: A Philosophy of the Interhuman*, ed. and trans. Maurice Friedman (New York: Harper & Row, 1965), 58.

2. Maurice Friedman, *Martin Buber: The Life of Dialogue* (London: Routledge & Kegan Paul, Chicago: University of Chicago Press, 1955), 97.

3. Maurice Friedman, *Encounter on the Narrow Ridge: A Life of Martin Buber* (New York: Paragon House, 1991), 460.

4. Maurice Friedman, born in 1921, died in his ninetieth year (on September 24, 2012), after this book was written, but before it was published.

5. Grete Schaeder, ed. and intro., *Martin Buber: Briefwechsel aus selben Jahrzehnten*, 3 vols., 1938–1965 (Heidelberg: Lambert Schneider: 1975).

3. On the Suspension of the Ethical

1. James William Walters quotes Buber in his book *Martin Buber and Feminist Ethics* (New York: Syracuse University Press, 2003), 53.

2. Martin Buber, *I and Thou*, 2nd ed., trans. Ronald Gregor Smith (New York: Charles Scribner's Sons, 1958), 135.

3. Martin Buber, *The Origin and Meaning of Hasidism*, trans. Maurice Friedman (New York: Harper Torchbooks, 1960), 136–37.

4. "Sacred versus Symbolic Religion: Abraham Joshua Heschel and Martin Buber," *Modern Judaism* 14 (Fall 1994): 213–31.

5. Maurice Friedman, *Martin Buber's Life and Work: The Later Years* (Detroit: Wayne State University Press, 1988), 138.

6. Martin Buber, *Eclipse of God* (New York: Harper & Brothers, 1952), 23.

7. Maurice Friedman, *Martin Buber: The Life of Dialogue* (Chicago: University of Chicago Press, 1955), 131.

4. Martin Buber's First Visit to America

1. Buber's beautiful little essay "Books and Men," which I have translated and included in Buber's book of collected essays *Pointing the Way*, will give the reader a further understanding of what Buber meant by this statement to me.

2. Martin Buber, *At the Turning* (New York: Farrar, Straus & Young, 1952), 48–49.

3. Martin Buber, *I and Thou*, 2nd ed., trans. Ronald Gregor Smith (New York: Charles Scribner's Sons, 1958), 135–36.

4. Maurice Friedman, *Abraham Joshua Heschel and Elie Wiesel: You Are My Witnesses* (New York: Farrar, Straus & Giroux, 1987), 146.

5. Maurice Friedman, *Martin Buber: The Life of Dialogue* (Chicago: University of Chicago Press, 1955), 224–25.

6. Martin Buber, *Eclipse of God* (New York: Harper & Brothers, 1952), 31–32.

7. Ibid., 35.

8. Ibid., 38.

9. Unpublished letter, quoted in Maurice Friedman, *Encounter on the Narrow Ridge: A Life of Martin Buber* (New York: Paragon House, 1991), 342.

10. Irving Howe, "Albert Camus: The Life of Dialogue," *Dissent* 8, no. 2 (April 1961): 210.

5. Sartre, Heidegger, Jung, and Scholem

1. Maurice Friedman, *Martin Buber's Life and Work: The Later Years* (Detroit: Wayne State University Press, 1988), 172–75.

2. See Martin Buber's *Eclipse of God* (New York: Humanities Press International), 69–71.

3. Friedman, *Martin Buber's Life and Work*, 165.

4. Buber, *Eclipse of God*, 124.

5. Ibid., 126.

6. Ibid., 129.

7. Ibid., 78–91.

8. Ibid.

9. Ibid.

10. Ibid.

11. Ibid.

12. Ibid.

13. The complete text of my notes of the Washington seminars on the unconscious and dreams is printed in Martin Buber, *A Believing Humanism: Gleanings*, trans. and intro. by Maurice Friedman (New York: Simon & Schuster, 1969), chapter on "The Unconscious," 153–73. It is well worth reading.

14. Buber, *Eclipse of God*, 78–91.

15. Ibid., 136–37.

16. Martin Buber, "Interpreting Hasidism," *Commentary* 36, no. 3 (1963): 218–25.

17. Martin Buber, *The Origin and Meaning of Hasidism*, trans. Maurice Friedman (New York: Harper Torchbooks, 1960), 254.

18. See Maurice Friedman, *A Dialogue with Hasidic Tales: Hallowing the Everyday* (New York: Human Sciences Press, 1988), 53.

6. The Life of Dialogue: Letters Following Buber's First Visit

1. Martin Buber, *At the Turning* (New York: Farrar, Straus, & Young, 1952), 61.

8. The Washington School of Psychiatry and the Buber-Rogers Dialogue

1. Martin Buber, *Good and Evil* (New York: Charles Scribner's Sons, 1952), 43.

10. Buber's Last Visit to America

1. See "Healing through Meeting: Dialogical Psychotherapy," in *Dialogically Speaking: Maurice Friedman's Interdisciplinary Humanism*, ed. Kenneth Paul Kramer (Eugene, Ore.: Pickwick, 2011), 219–36.

11. Interrogations and Responses: Letters Following Buber's Last Visit

1. Martin Buber, *The Knowledge of Man: A Philosophy of the Interhuman* (New York: Harper & Row, 1965).

2. *Philosophical Interrogations*, ed. Sydney and Beatrice Rome (New York: Holt, Rinehart, & Winston, 1964), 82.

3. See "The Image of Man and Moral Philosophy" in my 1967 book *To Deny Our Nothingness: Contemporary Images of Man* (Chicago: University of Chicago Press, 1984).

4. *Philosophical Interrogations*, 67.

5. Ibid., 111.

12. Our Stay in Jerusalem and Buber's Last Years

1. Maurice Friedman, "Walter Kaufmann's Mismeeting with Buber," *Judaism* 31, no. 2 (Spring 82): 229.

2. *The Philosophy of Martin Buber*, ed. Paul Arthur Schlipp and Maurice Friedman (LaSalle, Ill.: Open Court, 1967), 725–26.

3. Quoted in Maurice Friedman, *Encounter on the Narrow Ridge: A Life of Martin Buber* (New York: Paragon House, 1991), 419.

4. Friedman, *Martin Buber's Life and Work: The Later Years* (Detroit: Wayne State University Press, 1988), 330–31. Friedman's note for this quote appears on page 453 in which he says: "Letter from Charles Malik to Maurice Friedman, June 27, 1962."

Epilogue: Memorial Address

1. Address given at the Martin Buber Memorial Meeting, Park Avenue Synagogue, July 13, 1965, under the auspices of the American Friends of the Hebrew University.

2. Martin Buber, *Pointing the Way*, trans. Maurice Friedman (New York: Harper Torchbooks, 1957), 3ff.

3. Maurice Friedman, *Martin Buber's Life and Work: The Later Years* (Detroit: Wayne State University Press, 1988), 1:123.

4. Martin Buber, *Hasidism and Modern Man*, trans. Maurice Friedman (New York: Harper Torchbooks, 1958), 68.

5. Martin Buber, *The Knowledge of Man*, ed. and intro. Maurice Friedman, trans. Maurice Friedman and Ronald Gregor Smith (New York: Harper & Row, 1965), 183.

6. Martin Buber, *At the Turning*, (New York: Farrar, Straus, & Young, 1952), 62.

7. Martin Buber, *I and Thou*, 2nd ed., trans. R. G. Smith (New York: Charles Scribner's Sons, 1937/57), 136–37.

References

Buber, Martin. 1952. *At the Turning*. New York: Farrar, Straus, and Young.

———. 1957. *Eclipse of God: Studies in the Relation of Religion and Philosophy*. Translated by Maurice Friedman. New York: Harper Torchbooks.

———. 1957. *I and Thou*. 2nd ed. Translated by Ronald Gregor Smith. 1937. New York: Charles Scribner's Sons.

———. 1958. *Hasidism and Modern Man*. Translated by Maurice Friedman. New York: Harper Torchbooks.

———. 1960. *The Origin and Meaning of Hasidism*. Translated by Maurice Friedman. New York: Harper & Row.

———. 1965. *The Knowledge of Man: A Philosophy of the Interhuman*. Translated and edited by Maurice Friedman. New York: Harper & Row.

———. 1967. *Meetings*. Translated by Maurice Friedman. La Salle, Ill: Open Court Publishing.

———. 1967. *Pointing the Way: Collected Essays*. Translated and edited by Maurice Friedman. New York: Harper Torchbooks.

———. 1969. *A Believing Humanism: Gleanings*. Translated, with an Introduction and Explanatory Comments by Maurice Friedman. New York: Simon & Schuster.

Friedman, Maurice. 1955. *Martin Buber: The Life of Dialogue*. London: Routledge & Kegan Paul; Chicago: Univ. of Chicago Press.

———. 1963. *Problematic Rebel: An Image of Modern Man*. New York: Random House.

———. 1967. *To Deny Our Nothingness: Contemporary Images of Man*. New York: Dell Publishing.

———. 1988. *Martin Buber's Life and Work: The Later Years*. Detroit: Wayne State Univ. Press.

————. 1991. *Encounter on the Narrow Ridge: A Life of Martin Buber.* New York: Paragon House.

Kramer, Kenneth Paul, ed. 2011. *Dialogically Speaking: Maurice Friedman's Interdisciplinary Humanism.* Eugene, OR: Pickwick Publications.

Index